# Walking
# IN THE WILL
# OF GOD

❖ STEVE MCVEY ❖

HARVEST HOUSE PUBLISHERS

EUGENE, OREGON

*Cover by Left Coast Design, Portland, Oregon*

*Cover photo © Steve Terrill*

**WALKING IN THE WILL OF GOD**
Copyright © 2009 by Steve McVey
Eugene, Oregon 97402
www.harvesthousepublishers.com

Library of Congress Cataloging-in-Publication Data

McVey, Steve, 1954-
Walking in the will of God / Steve McVey.
    p. cm.
ISBN 978-0-7369-2639-3 (pbk.)
1. Christian life. 2. God (Christianity)—Will. I. Title.
BV4501.3.M396 2009
248.4—dc22

2008038743

**Printed in the United States of America**

13 14 15 16 17 / VP-NI / 10 9 8 7 6 5 4 3

To "John,"
whose courage and commitment make him
more like the apostle Paul than any other
man I've ever known.

I pray for you daily.

# ❊ CONTENTS ❊

# The End of Agonizing

"I don't know what to do," Trent told me after I had spoken at his church one Sunday. "There's a good chance I might be offered a position with a new company where my salary would be almost twice what it is now, which of course is very attractive. On the other hand, I love the job I have now, and I'm afraid to give it up for something new that I could end up not enjoying nearly as much.

"If I could only *know* what God's will is for me, I would do it without hesitating. I'm just not sure. If I could be sure, I'd be willing to go either way. I just need to know."

Trent's situation and question are very much like those we all seem to face regularly in our lives. We want to do the will of God. We certainly don't want to miss it, but how can a person know for sure what God's will is in any given situation? The idea of making a wrong choice, which could put us on the wrong track in life, is a scenario none of us want to see come about. How, though, can we be sure? As I travel and speak in various places, this is a question I am often asked.

There are probably many reasons why this question weighs so heavily on people's minds. Maybe it does on yours. In my years of talking to believers, I've found that their concerns about finding the will of God fall into three main areas.

**Big reason #1.** To start with, there's *the burden of simply having to decide.* The consequences of our choices can be so many and so devastating that we naturally feel anxiety over our ability to know and do the right thing. Many people are like Trent in their perspective. On the one hand, they know what their life is like right now, and there's nothing happening that would motivate them to seek a change. It's not that hard to make a decision for change if the circumstances you're in aren't what you want, but when everything is okay it becomes easy to follow the "leave well enough alone" mind-set. In one of our discussions about his options, Trent said to me, "Maybe I just shouldn't rock the boat." This perspective betrays a subtle fear about change in life, but Trent certainly isn't in a minority here. Underlying fears have paralyzed many people, keeping them from moving forward in life.

On the other hand, these same people want to be open to the possibility that God may have bigger and better things in store for them. If that's what is going on when they are faced with the potential of a move, they don't want to miss out. So they find themselves at a place where making a decision is, in and of itself, a stressful place to be. *Do I do it or not do it?* Just in itself, that's often a challenging question.

> It's all up to *Him*. The word for that kind of situation is…grace!

**Big reason #2.** How to understand God's will also often triggers a sense of anxiety in people because of *misconceptions regarding what God wants and expects from us.* If we have wrong ideas about expectations He may have for us, we will be stuck when it comes to confidently making life-altering decisions. After all, we certainly don't want to mess up. Some people think they have to find God's will by determining the exact spot in the universe where He wants them to stand so they can do the exact thing He has in mind for them. To make matters worse, they think it is up to them to figure it all out for themselves. What a burden! That kind of viewpoint will cause anybody to be nervous and tentative about life.

As you move through this book, you will see that God never intended for us to live like that. In the chapters ahead, you are going to find yourself being set free from fears about the future based on decisions you make today. You will be pleased to discover how to make choices grounded in a calm confidence that your loving Father isn't going to let you make some foolish decision now that is going to wreck His perfect plan for you later. God is bigger than you, and He loves you enough to make sure that you discover His plan for you. It's up to Him, not you, to make it happen. Take note of that statement: It's all up to *Him.* The word for that kind of situation is…grace!

*Grace* means *He* does what needs to be done and you simply live in faith, as the beneficiary of His actions. You just respond to Him. That's it. Knowing how to do that is what this book is about.

**Big reason #3.** Additionally, many people are stressed out over knowing God's will due to *the common belief that His plan is mysterious*—so mysterious that it takes some kind of miraculous breakthrough in order to find exactly what it is. If we should miss that plan, we fear that it is gone forever and we will never recover from the loss. No wonder we feel anxiety and pressure! However, that's simply not the way it is and, again, you'll come to understand the truth about this issue as you move ahead in your reading.

It amazes me how many Christians live with the fear they are going to miss God's best for their lives. The encouraging truth is, God *does* have a specific plan for you that He wants to fulfill through you. The best news, though, is that it's not up to you to figure out that plan. It's up to Him to *reveal* it to you. And He will!

You may find what you're going to read here about knowing God's will to be different from what you've heard or read on the subject in the past. This book is a grace-book, and that perspective is going to make all the difference in how you perceive and pursue God's will for your life.

As Christians walking in grace, we don't have to agonize about whether or not we are going to miss God's will. Our God is completely capable of making His plan clear to us and then enabling us to fulfill that plan. Not only is He capable of showing us, He is *eager* for us to know His will. Those two facts ensure a winning combination!

Are you ready to discover how you can confidently walk in the will of God? Before you begin the first chapter, why not pause now and ask your Father to enable you to set aside any faulty preconceived ideas about how to know His will? Ask Him to reveal biblical truth to you concerning this subject.

It's true: Your Father has a plan in mind for you. It's a great plan, because great plans are the only kind He can design. Do you want to discover and do what He has designed for you? Open your mind and your heart, and let's begin with a basic truth that deals with understanding who is in control of your life.

CHAPTER 1

# Remember Who Is in Charge

"TRENT, I WANT TO ASK YOU A QUESTION," I said to the friend I introduced a few pages ago. "How did you get the job you have now?"

"Well, it was really strange in some ways," he answered. "My sister was dating a guy who worked for the company I'm at now. She happened to mention to him one day that I was looking for a job in computer graphics. He told her that, just within the past few days, he had heard something about their computer graphics guy resigning to go back to school."

"So you sent in your résumé?" I asked.

"I didn't have to," Trent continued. "My sister's boyfriend told his boss about my degree in computer graphics and gave me a glowing recommendation. The boss asked him to have me call for an interview. The first time he saw my résumé was when I handed it to him in person."

"And, as they say, the rest is history?" I asked.

"Yep, that's pretty much it. He liked me from the get-go and asked me to come back for a second interview with his boss, who also liked me enough that he offered me the job on the spot."

"Wow, that's great," I continued. "I'm curious—is your sister still dating that guy?"

"No, they only went out a few times."

"Hmm...sounds like God may have been more interested in you having a great job than your sister having a great date," I said with a chuckle.

As we talked, I encouraged Trent to realize that, just as God had worked through his circumstances to get him into his current job, He could do the same thing with this opportunity. "God stopped your sister from going forward with the guy she was dating, right?" I asked him.

"Yes," he answered.

"And God caused you to start a new job?"

"That's right."

"So it sounds like, as the saying goes, the stops and steps of a person are ordered by the Lord," I continued.

As we discussed it further, Trent began to see the big picture. The fact is, it isn't up to us to make things happen or to keep things from happening because, when it comes to how our life unfolds, it really isn't about us. *God* is in control. The best part of that truth is, He will always work out the details of our life for His own glory and our highest good. That's just the kind of God He is!

> You aren't the one who has to be sure that you do His will. That's *His* role.

To put it another way, yours is a graced life, which means that God assumes the responsibility for revealing His will to you. It isn't a matter of being smart enough, careful enough, or even spiritual enough to figure it all out. *You* aren't the one who has to be sure that you do His will. That's *His* role. As I've already pointed out, that's why it's called *grace*. He does it all.

## Is Anyone Really "Independent"?

In the Psalms, there is a great passage that assures us of God's ability to see to it that we find out and follow His will.

The LORD has established His throne in the heavens,
And His sovereignty rules over all.
Bless the LORD, you His angels,
Mighty in strength, who perform His word,
Obeying the voice of His word!
Bless the LORD, all you His hosts,
You who serve Him, doing His will.
Bless the LORD, all you works of His,
In all places of His dominion;
Bless the LORD, O my soul.

—Psalm 103:19-22

David tells us in this passage that God is able to cause us to fulfill His will, and that His will *will* be done. Look again at verse 19: "The LORD has established His throne in the heavens, and His sovereignty rules over all." What a difference from how many people see things! The philosophy of the world suggests that man somehow determines his own destiny based on *his* abilities, *his* goals, and *his* self-confidence in achieving those goals. The Psalm quoted above also says,

As for man, his days are like grass;
As a flower of the field, so he flourishes.
When the wind has passed over it, it is no more,
And its place acknowledges it no longer.

—Psalm 103:15-16

It is foolish for any of us to think we can determine our own destiny apart from God![At best, man apart from God is a wilting flower—here today and gone tomorrow.]

And yet, many still believe they can independently decide their own destiny. You can go to any bookstore and find shelves filled with books telling you that you create your own destiny. These self-help books have gone so far as to tell us that if our minds can conceive it and we can believe it, then we can achieve it. How absurd. Only Almighty God has that kind of sovereign power. Jesus told His followers, "Apart from

Me you can do nothing" (John 15:5). However, it is equally true that "I can do all things *through Christ* who strengthens me" (Philippians 4:13 NKJV).

The world tells us that we, in and of ourselves, can do anything. The Christian knows better. [The value of anything we do apart from Christ adds up to nothing.] However, as we depend upon Him and recognize His authority and guidance over our lives, we can accomplish supernatural feats in this life.

We understand that God has given us our lives and has a unique purpose for each of us. The question for most Christians, therefore, is not *whether* God has a plan for us. The issue revolves around *how we can know* what that plan is, and *how we can live* in the center of God's will for our lives.

Let's begin at the center, the appropriate starting place in any scenario of life, by considering a fundamental question.

## Just Who Is in Charge?

Anywhere you go in life, somebody has to be in charge. If there is absolutely no ruling presence in a situation, chaos exists. We know that God did not create, and does not promote, chaos. He is a God of logic, reason, and order, and He created a world of order. This world and its inhabitants don't live in some sort of helter-skelter, nonsensical realm without order or purpose. God is the One in charge, and the Scripture says that His reign extends over *all*. Don't be deceived about this point: "All" means *all*. There is no hidden place in this immense universe where God does not have control even to the minutest detail. He is God, and He is supreme.

As Trent began to understand this truth, he decided to go ahead and finish the interview process for the new job possibility. During the course of the process, he began to sense a few personality issues in his potential new boss that didn't sit well with him. That was enough for him to realize he didn't want to make the move.

Later, when he explained to me what had happened, he said, "I initially felt a little disappointed that the job wasn't the chance of a lifetime I had hoped it would be. On the other hand, the process did encourage me by helping me to see that, just like you and I discussed, [ God can stop us from moving in a wrong direction just as easily as He can start us moving in a right direction." ]

In the end, though it didn't lead to a new job, Trent was thankful for the experience. Through it, the truth was more firmly established in his mind that God really is in control. It's not up to us to make anything in life happen. Our only role is to calmly trust Him, knowing that, when the time comes for something to happen to move us further toward the fulfillment of His will for us, He will see to it that we are in the right place at the right time and will make the right decision.

To think we are the captains of our own destiny is not only a lack of faith—it is a symptom of pride. God's plan is that we yield ourselves to Him in humble submission, knowing He will guide us into His will.

## Nobody Is Bigger than God

The fourth chapter of Daniel records the "education" of a totally arrogant king, Nebuchadnezzar of Babylon. Having been firmly put in his place by God, he humbly acknowledges that the Lord alone is sovereign.

> All the inhabitants of the earth are accounted as nothing,
>   But He does according to His will in the host of heaven
> And among the inhabitants of earth;
>   And no one can ward off His hand
> Or say to Him, "What have You done?"
>
> —Daniel 4:35

God is going to get His way. Make no mistake about it; He is in complete charge of everything. If He isn't, then He is in charge of nothing, in which case we might as well "eat, drink and be merry, for tomorrow we die." The fact is, He *is* in control. He is in charge of the universe and everything in it.

Psalm 22:28 says, "He rules over the nations." God sets up

kingdoms; He overthrows empires; He determines the course of dynasties, according to what best pleases Him.

We are often impressed, even awed, at what we call human achievement. We can see examples from ancient history, like the empires of Alexander or Caesar. Contemporary examples abound in nations, corporations, or organizations that are prominent in the news. But none of them impress God.

> You have rebuked the nations, You have destroyed the wicked;
>> You have blotted out their name forever and ever.
> The enemy has come to an end in perpetual ruins,
>> And You have uprooted the cities;
> The very memory of them has perished.
> But the LORD abides forever; He has established
>> His throne for judgment,
> And He will judge the world in righteousness;
>> He will execute judgment for the people with equity.
>
> —Psalm 9:5-8

As I've traveled the world speaking over the past years, I've seen the evidence of man's greatest achievements. I've stood on the Great Wall of China. I've walked through the Taj Mahal in India. I've seen the ancient ruins of the Incas in Peru and the Mayas in Mexico. In Japan and Korea, I've stood outside temples made from pure gold. Across the world, on every inhabited continent, there have been many "great civilizations," some of which lasted hundreds of years. They once were impressive; now they are neglected ruins. Things made by humans pass away, but God and His Word are forever.

It's no wonder the apostle Paul referred to God as "the blessed and only Sovereign, the King of kings and Lord of lords" (1 Timothy 6:15). God asks nobody's advice or permission about anything. He does what He wants and, as much as we may wish otherwise, He doesn't have to explain His reasoning to us.

Somebody bigger than us is in charge! Any meaningful discussion about knowing and doing God's will must begin with this understanding. This leads to two foundational truths that will guide us in our investigation. We will examine the first here, and then take up the second in the next chapter. Both of these truths point us toward God, not man.

## God's Rule over Everything Includes *You*

To say that I'm not very good with directions would be an understatement. In fact, I often tell people, "I know left from right, but I don't speak compass." It is ridiculously bad—once, when somebody in a strange town mocked me for not knowing which direction was east by reminding me that it's where the sun comes up, I jokingly responded, "I haven't been in this town when the sun came up!" I remind myself that there are other things I'm good at, which proves I'm not a complete moron.

On one such occasion, I was trying to find my way to a location in a town I'd never visited. Somebody had given me directions, and I was driving along trying to find the spot. I had been told to begin in a certain direction, turn south, and continue for six miles to my destination. My male ego wouldn't let me admit that I didn't know one direction from another.

He's in charge. That's a fact you can't afford to miss.

After exiting the road and driving for ten miles, I knew I had done something wrong. I eventually discovered that instead of turning south, I had turned north. Maybe it's some sort of mental wiring that has short-circuited in me. Whatever the cause, that old, familiar feeling of being lost began to rise in me yet again, despite the fact I had tried so hard.

### *Do You Need to Make a Turnaround?*

I had meant well. I was sincere, but I could never succeed by going in the wrong direction. That's the way it is in determining the will of

God for our lives. If we fail to look toward His sovereign control—if we choose to look in another direction—we will never find the satisfaction of living confidently in His will. We will never be sure about knowing His plan for our lives if we don't realize that the Lord Himself is the source for revealing His will.

What do we mean when we say that God is *sovereign?* In defining *sovereignty,* the dictionary uses descriptions like "supreme excellence"… "supreme power"…"freedom from external control; autonomy; controlling influence." All of these are true to the ultimate degree when it comes to God. He's in charge. That's a fact you can't afford to miss.

Why do we begin this subject with the sovereignty of God? Because it is unavoidable and inescapable! If God rules the universe and everything in it—*and you are in it*—then God's rule extends over *you* too.

I once heard somebody tell about the time he'd talked to a trapeze artist in the circus. He had watched the man swing high above the ground, doing twists and turns, hanging upside down, and doing other amazing tricks. What surprised him was the perspective of the trapeze artist about the net below.

"I guess the fact that there is a net beneath you is something you're always aware of," he remarked to the circus performer.

"Why so?" asked the man.

"Well, I'm sure that when you're up there doing such daring tricks, you are constantly aware you could fall," he continued.

"No, not at all," the performer answered. "I never think about falling. In fact, I don't even think about the net. I know it's there, but I don't think about it. I used to, but now I guess the unconscious awareness that it would catch me if I were to fall just gives me the courage and boldness to attempt things I never would have tried otherwise."

This man didn't do his circus routine thinking constantly about the possibility of falling. The underlying awareness of the safety net emboldened him to do his thing with confidence. He was empowered by that perspective.

The fact is, we have a safety net under us because we have the Holy

Spirit in us. The Spirit of Christ is our internal Guide. This guarantees that we are able to walk in the will of God. When you understand the meaning of grace, it takes the pressure off.]

We don't have to go through life praying, "Catch me if I fall," over and over again. When we come to rest in the reality that our loving and sovereign God is always there for us, it instills in us a boldness to live more courageously and daringly than we would ever live otherwise. Knowing that God is in control isn't primarily about knowing what would happen if we fall. It's about learning to live life with gusto—or "more abundantly," to use the words of Jesus (see John 10:10).]

You don't have to be afraid that you will fall by missing God's will, because it is not up to you to find it or to fulfill it. You can relax about the idea that you may fall out of it. *It's up to God to reveal His will to us and to keep us in it,* and He will do it. If God rules everything, and God rules you, then you don't have to worry about getting out of His will.

## The Whole Creation Is Glad He Made It

God rules as Creator of all things. In Revelation 4:11 we can read one of the hymns that will be sung in heaven, words that are being sung in heaven even now:

> Worthy are You, our Lord and our God, to receive glory and honor and power; for You created all things, and because of Your will they existed, and were created.

What a song! God willed the physical universe to exist, and so it did. Why did God create the universe? Proverbs 16:4 tells us that "the LORD has made everything for His own purpose." He did it for one simple reason—because it was what He wanted. The psalmist said, "He spoke, and it was done; He commanded, and it stood fast" (Psalm 33:9).

The universe exists because it was the will of God. The stars don't hang up there on nothing. They are held in place by the will of an omnipotent God. The tide at the beach doesn't just coincidentally stop at its boundaries and return to the sea. It is ordered back by divine design. The earth isn't spinning on its axis because of its own momentum. That's the will of God at work. He designed it that way. The inanimate world in which we live conforms to the will of God.

This is why many of the psalms celebrate God's creation: from the stars and planets to the earth and sea; from the cycles of the seasons to the living creatures. As John Calvin wrote, "There is not one little blade of grass, there is no color in this world that is not intended to make men rejoice." He liked to refer to nature as "the theater of God's glory." Martin Luther felt the same, and remarked, "But I can't understand what must be in a man's mind if he doesn't feel seriously that there is a God when he sees the sun rise."

These believers are responding to God's self-revelation in creation. They are following the example of David, who wrote, "The heavens are telling of the glory of God; and their expanse is declaring the work of His hands" (Psalm 19:1). These are examples of the only proper response to seeing a glimpse of the greatness of God, which is to bow in humble worship.

## He's Not Worried that Things Will Go Awry

All these things exist and occur simply because they are God's will. But not only is He Creator of all things; He rules as *Sustainer* of all things. In contrast, *Deism* is the belief that "God" somehow started up this whole universe, but since then has left it to run on its own; that He "wound it up, turned it loose, and let it go." Now He's just watching it run down. That's not what the Christian believes, and that's not what the Bible teaches.

The writer of Hebrews asserts that not only did the Son of God create the world, but He also "upholds all things by the word of His power" (Hebrews 1:3). In the same vein, Paul says of Christ that "in Him all things hold together" (Colossians 1:17). God did not create the world, set it in motion, and walk away, waiting for it to run out of steam. The Word of God declares that God is *actively involved* in the ongoing affairs of the world.

Isaiah 46:9-10 says,

> I am God, and there is no other;
>   I am God, and there is no one like Me,
> Declaring the end from the beginning,
>   And from ancient times things which have not
>     been done,
> Saying, "My purpose will be established,
>   And I will accomplish all My good pleasure."

If God has declared the end from the beginning, then He is the Lord of history and has planned it all. "History" is truly *His story*. He says He will carry out all His will on this planet. To hear some people talk, you'd think God was sitting on His throne in heaven, rocking back and forth and fighting off an anxiety attack about what's going on in the world. But that conception is completely foreign to what the Bible teaches. God is absolutely sovereign, sovereign over every person, and He will use every person who ever lived to accomplish the Divine Plan He has for this universe.

## God Is Even Sovereign over Evil

"Hold on a minute!" Loren said to me one day. "You don't really mean to say that God will use everybody, do you? There have been many wicked people in the world. Are you saying that God could use a man like Hitler or other monstrous people to accomplish His purpose?"

"Loren, it really comes down to one question," I responded. "Is God in control or is He not?"

"But God can't do evil!" Loren countered. "He gave man a free will."

"So are you suggesting that man sometimes does things that get the best of God and leave Him on the losing side?" I persevered. "Loren, make no mistake about it—God can't do evil. It isn't in His nature. However, He has chosen to allow evil to exist while He weaves it into

His greater purposes. Man is always responsible for the evil he chooses to do, and yet God remains in total control of the overall plan. Both are true at the same time."

I think Loren's problem was that he wanted to make sense of it all. But that's just not possible sometimes in this world. His argument for man's "free will" is a weak one when compared to the biblical teaching of a sovereign God who is in total control. When it comes down to who ultimately wins—man's will or God's word—I'll go with God's word every time.

### Don't Give Free Will Too Much Credit

The truth is, this whole idea of man's free will is overrated. By that, I mean that no man or woman who has ever been born is going to make a decision that trumps God's eternal purposes. When it is all said and done, whatever happens is what God wanted to happen. Otherwise, God has made His desires subservient to man's desires. God doing what man wants? The very idea is a slap in the face of His sovereignty.

When I look at events like the Nazi Holocaust, or the 9/11 attacks, or other horrible things that happen in this world, I can make no more sense out of them than anybody else. The fact is, though, we don't *have* to make

> When it is all said and done, we will be left with a God who was never blindsided by anything.

sense out of them. What we can do is to trust God in the midst of them. When this world has ended and we see things from the perspective of the One who is "all in all," it will all make sense then. For now, however, all we can do is trust. To insist on more than trust is to insist on control, and we aren't in control—God is. That fact shouldn't disturb us. To the contrary, it should encourage us.

Speaking of evil people, consider Judas. In Scripture he is called "the son of perdition"—literally, the son of hell. If we had been witness to what Judas did and then saw the resulting crucifixion of Jesus, there is no way we could have come to the conclusion that it was God's will, but it was. God used even the evil choice Judas made, didn't He? The most evil act of betrayal in history helped bring about the most important event in human history—our salvation in Jesus Christ. As much as anybody who has ever lived, the life of Judas shows that there is no evil person or evil circumstance that can frustrate God in His eternal plan.

We neither have to defend or explain what God allows in this life. Somehow, when it is all said and done, we will be left with a God who was never blindsided by anything that happened throughout the history of this world. To the contrary, He will have somehow fit together all the pieces, from the most beautiful to the most ugly, into the panorama of the ages He has designed.

## Nobody Scares God

God isn't intimidated by evil. Nor is He reacting to evil men by putting out fires they've started. He is bigger than that. It is no problem in the slightest for Him to turn evil around and use it creatively to accomplish His will.

Think about the other people who put Jesus on the cross. It was unspeakable evil in action, but God worked it into the fabric of His great tapestry. It fit right in with His sovereign plan for the universe. Out of the depths of such evil, God worked the greatest good man has ever known!

In a way that our finite minds can't grasp, human responsibility and divine sovereignty held hands and walked together when Jesus died. As the apostle Peter speaks of Jesus Christ during his sermon on the Day of Pentecost, he affirms how both fit together:

> This Man, delivered over by the predetermined plan and foreknowledge of God, you nailed to the cross by the hands of godless men and put Him to death. But God raised Him up again (Acts 2:23-24).

Do you see how the two fit together? Human beings were completely responsible for crucifying the Son of God. "You nailed [Him] to the cross," Peter said. But God was sovereign over even this, and in fact, had planned it before the foundation of the world: Christ was "delivered over by the predetermined plan and foreknowledge of God." We do have an awesome God!

So what about all the evil people in the world? They don't intimidate God, and they cannot evade God's rule over them. The Bible is clear that even evil will one day bow in submission to God's sovereign rule over His creation.

## Everyone Will Own Up to God's Sovereignty

Concerning all moral beings—evil people and faithful believers alike, and angelic beings, both good and evil—God has determined "that at the name of Jesus every knee will bow, of those who are in heaven and on earth and under the earth, and that every tongue will confess that Jesus Christ is Lord, to the glory of God the Father" (Philippians 2:10-11).

Evil people cannot and will not thwart God's plan. At the proper time, all without exception will acknowledge the sovereign God and His Son Jesus Christ—the only difference being that some do it now, while others will do it later. But at the end of the day, *all* will bow and confess.

God is sovereign. I repeat myself, and I do it purposely, to help counter the resistance I know by experience is in so many people's minds. Nothing catches God by surprise. *Nothing.* There has never been an occasion where something slipped past Him so that He had to come up with a "Plan B." God has never once said, "Oops," or asked, "*Now* what am I going to do?"

Remember, God created *time itself.* He is transcendent. He stands above time, over time, so that He sees the end from the beginning and everything between. In His eternal Now, He knows every decision made by every man and woman who ever lived or will ever live. He sees every event that will unfold. And from the perspective of eternity,

He is able to work in such a way that every action that takes place in the universe, from beginning to end, will contribute toward the fulfillment of His sovereign plan.

It may seem strange that I begin a study on knowing and doing the will of God with this emphasis on His sovereignty, but this has to be the starting place. I am laying the essential foundation upon which you can build a house of faith, a foundation from which you can know the will of God with certainty and be able to carry it out with enthusiasm.

As we proceed, keep the statement I have made in mind: God rules the universe and all that is in it...*and you are in it!* God rules. He rules over everything, and that means you don't have to be fearful. I meet so many Christians who are afraid. They ask, "Pray for me that I don't miss the will of God." I usually answer by asking, "Is your heart directed toward the Lord? Are you depending on Christ? Are you resting in Him?"

"Yes," they answer.

"Do you know that Jesus Christ is your very Life?"

"Yes."

"So then, what are you worrying about?" I ask. "You have a sovereign God who is in control of every event that happens in this universe. You have the life of Jesus Christ in you to empower you to do the will of the Father. You have the Holy Spirit in you to guide you into His will. What are you worried about?"

I often think that if we would give the Lord as much credit for His capacity to keep us *in* His will as we do our enemy, the devil, for his ability to influence us to fall *out* of God's will, we could move forward through life with a lot more boldness and confidence!

Why is it that some people are not comforted by the knowledge that God is sovereign and that He is in control of all things? People sometimes privately wonder, *What if His purposes for me aren't good?*

*What if* this *happens or what if* that *happens? How can I know He has my best interests at heart?*

Those questions point to the topic of the next chapter. The door that leads to our conscious experience of God's will swings on this hinge. Though God is in charge and that's an objective fact, in order to feel the truth of that fact in your own experience, you have to swing the door wide open on this hinge. What is it? *Trust*—a small word with huge ramifications.

## ❧ G. R. A. C. E. GROUP QUESTIONS ❧

A G.R.A.C.E. (Giving & Receiving Affirmative Christian Encouragement) Group is any gathering of people who meet together to encourage and strengthen each other in the grace of God. Use these discussion questions, which you'll find at the end of each chapter, to facilitate further learning and discussion. As you consider them, the truths of this book will be worked more deeply into your life. If you aren't a member of a small group, answer the questions on your own by writing a brief response to each one.

1.  Read Psalm 103:19. How would you define the word "all" in that verse? Does God rule over everything in this world? In what sense does He "rule" over the people and affairs we encounter in this life, when it seems that so many wrong choices are made in this world?

2.  Have you ever read any self-help books that teach that all people are capable of determining their own destinies? Which one of the

books you may have read comes to mind? What was the main message of that book? How does this chapter contradict the secular approach to accomplishing great things in our lives? Read Isaiah 31:1, Psalm 20:7, and Zechariah 4:6. What do these verses say about this subject?

3. Put Daniel 4:35 in your own words. Write a version of the verse in such a way that it makes application to the circumstances of your own life.

4. When we believe that the sovereignty of God over our lives is a safety net for us, how might this change the way we live? Read Psalm 48:14. How might that truth affect a person who is deciding where to attend school? Which career path to pursue? Who to marry? Which local church to participate in? What is another verse that encourages us about God's sovereignty over the details of our lives?

5. Describe an evil event in which you have found yourself involved. How does the fact that God is in charge of everything apply to what you experienced? Can you see the divine hand of God in the midst of the situation? What are we to do when we can't find any evidence at all of God's presence in the midst of evil in our lives? Read Nahum 1:3 and explain how the last half of the verse applies to situations in our lives when evil has been imposed upon us.

6. How would you describe the tension between the choices God allows people to make and the fact that He is ultimately in control of everything that happens? How does Proverbs 16:9 apply to that seeming tension?

# CHAPTER 2

# Decide Who You're Going To Trust

"IF I HAD WAITED TEN MINUTES more to leave home, I wouldn't have been there when that other car ran the red light. But now our car is wrecked!" Barry said to his wife. As things had turned out, nobody was hurt, but the other driver didn't have car insurance. Barry was glad to be okay, but he was seriously stressed about the amount of money the accident would cost their family.

He rehashed the situation, thinking again and again about how the whole thing could have been avoided if he hadn't chosen to skip eating the bowl of cereal he normally had in the morning. In his mind, the simple choice to leave a few minutes earlier than usual had led to the unwelcomed situation.

Though he is a Christian, Barry was blind at that moment to a crucial biblical truth: We don't live in a universe of chaos and randomness. Things don't just happen. As we saw in chapter 1, the God who made all things is absolutely sovereign, and He is working out His plan for all things, including you. There is nothing that will ever happen in your life that will take God by surprise. So, once you can rest in the truth of His sovereignty, you are ready to move on to another important truth.

## Our All-Powerful God Can Be Trusted

We can trust God to guide our lives, even when things happen that make no sense. You can *trust* Him. If God has created the universe and directs its course to ensure that it accomplishes His purpose for its existence, you can be assured He will direct you, the one He has created in the very image of Jesus Christ.

If He controls all the events that happen in the world…if He controls the inanimate objects of the world…if He controls the boundaries of the tide, and controls the movements of the planets and the earth revolving on its axis…if He controls the actions of living things, such as the birds that migrate south in the winter, the complex organization observed in an anthill or beehive, and the social behaviors of apes…what does He not control?

If God is carrying out His will in the lives of ants and apes, of bees and birds, you can rest in the fact that He is going to work out His will in *your* life. Don't flatter yourself by thinking that you're big enough to stop it!

Ephesians 2:10 says, "We are His workmanship, created in Christ Jesus for good works, which God prepared beforehand so that we would walk in them." [You have been *created* with a plan in mind, and the One who made the plan is the same One who will see that it is carried out in the way He intends.

> God's will for you isn't something He is putting together while you're stumbling through this life.

God created you in His image. He breathed His life into you. It is His desire to manifest His glory through *you*, His beloved child. Ephesians 2:10 teaches us that even before He made the world, God planned the good things we would do that would bring glory to Him.

God's will for you isn't something He is putting together while you're stumbling through this life. He had it all figured out before you even showed up here—and He has been working through your circumstances to bring you to the fulfillment of that plan all along. Therefore, the key to your moving through life with a sense of divine destiny is directly related to your trust in Him.

Barry couldn't make sense out of why God would allow him to get in a wreck, but the fact is, there *was* a reason. Who knows what that reason was? Maybe he would have had a more serious accident later that was prevented by this one. Maybe the delay redirected his actions in a way that allowed him to be used by God that day in a specific way that would otherwise have been missed. Maybe through the accident God was teaching him a valuable spiritual lesson. Barry didn't understand why the wreck happened, but God did. The possibilities are unlimited as to why God would have allowed it to happen at that moment, but you can be sure that the incident fit in with God's plan.

The reality of the matter is this: Barry didn't have an "accident," because there are no accidents. Our God directs our steps. Nothing happens in our lives outside of His control. Anything and everything you will ever experience in this world happens for a purpose. In a way that we often will not understand, every detail of life guides us toward the fulfillment of the divine plan our Father has for us. We take a big step toward understanding something about the will of God for our lives when we give ourselves over to Him, recognizing that everything in our circumstances can be used by Him to move us toward knowing and doing His will. That's true whether circumstances make sense to us or not.

## Settle the Trust Issue Now

If you want to consciously experience God's will for your life, it is important to first believe that *He* wants to see His plan for your life played out through you even more than you do. It all boils down to what you believe about Him. Once, when the disciples asked Jesus what they should do in order to do the work of God, Jesus answered them, "This is the work of God, that you *believe* in Him whom He has sent" (John 6:29).

To move ahead in boldly embracing God's will for your life, you'll need to settle the issue of who you're going to trust—Him or yourself. Don't skim past this section without thinking about that—*Who are you going to trust?*

To trust in <u>ourselves</u> will lead only to insecurity, fear, and a desperate attempt to be in control of things that, in reality, we cannot control. To trust in our loving Father <u>relieves</u> us of all that. Why would any of us choose to depend on ourselves, when we have the assurance that He is willing and able to lead us each step of the way?

You don't have to worry about missing God's best for your life. He is determined to lead you into His best for you. You can believe this—He *will* do it.

## Have Faith in a Person, Not a Procedure or Power

The writer of Hebrews said, "Without faith it is impossible to please Him, for he who comes to God must believe that He is and that He is a rewarder of those who seek Him" (Hebrews 11:6). That statement speaks clearly to the importance of faith in our daily walk. But then comes the question, "How do we make our faith grow?" Most of us have times when it seems like our faith is very flimsy. How can our faith grow stronger in those moments?

The Bible says that "faith comes from hearing, and hearing by the word of Christ" (Romans 10:17). We have to decide to believe what God has said no matter how strong our faith may seem at the time. The answer is to focus on Him, not on what we believe the strength of our faith might be. The issue isn't how strong our faith is, but how strong our God is.

### A Real-Life Man of Faith

In Romans 4, Abraham takes center stage in Scripture as a prime example of what faith looks like in action. Although he lived long ago, Abraham had the same kind of challenge we have as we go through life and face various trials. He had to decide how to respond when what he saw with his eyes didn't match what God had said. It is precisely at those moments our faith is tested.

Paul describes Abraham's response in Romans 4:20-21: "With respect to the promise of God, he did not waver in unbelief but grew strong in faith, giving glory to God, and being fully assured that what God had promised, He was able also to perform."

Now that's an interesting statement, Paul. Are we talking about the same man? I'm thinking of the one who had to have God tell him again and again that He was going to follow through on what He had said. The man who had relations with a servant girl because he was convinced his biological clock was quickly winding down. That's the guy who you're saying didn't waver in unbelief?

"That's the one," Paul would answer. Faith doesn't mean we have to feel strong and confident at every moment. It means we just keep clinging to God, even through the highs and lows of our day-to-day experiences.

Abraham had his ups and downs in both the consistency and strength of his faith. Through it all, our God of grace kept causing his faith to grow. Abraham's own emotions ran back and forth from desperate fear to calm confidence, but God kept being God throughout the whole process. The only thing that kept Abraham from completely giving up was God's repeated assurances that He would keep His word.

Think of it this way: The man who today is known as "the father of faith" didn't always feel confident about how things would turn out. Based on the understanding of faith many in the modern church have, Abraham blew it. By this modern definition, he appeared to be about as inconsistent as a person could be.

It's true—in the mix of his circumstances Abraham demonstrated confidence at one moment and cowardice at another, but at the end of the day, he proved that God can be trusted. He believed God. His faith was wobbly and weak at times, but he clung to God's promises anyway. In this way he's a great example. You don't have to feel like a spiritual superstar to have faith. Just keep clinging to the Superstar who lives inside you. He has enough faith for both of you.

### The "Me-First" Kind of Faith

Religious legalism distorts the meaning of faith by treating it as if it were some sort of spiritual currency we can use with God to get what we want from Him. Many people think they have to possess a faith that is defined by constantly having strong feelings of assurance and consistent thoughts of certainty that things are going to turn out the way they want.

Danny and I were talking one day about how depressed the real-estate market was. The subject had great importance to him because he worked for a mortgage company. "Management at our company has already laid off about a third of our employees," he told me.

"Are you concerned about your job?" I asked.

"No," he answered. "I'm believing God for my job. He knows that our oldest son, Dave, is in college now and that Ted will start in the fall. If I've ever needed a steady income, it's now. They're telling us at work that we're fighting to stay afloat, but I think everything will be okay."

"I hope so," I answered.

"I don't hope—I'm *believing* in faith," he responded with a little irritation in his voice.

I immediately knew I had said something wrong. I know Danny well enough to understand that his view of faith requires that he affirm with gusto that things will turn out the way he wants. From his perspective, to acknowledge that a different outcome is even a remote possibility translates to a lack of faith. Faith means believing it will happen the way we're praying it will happen. To him, it's that simple.

### "I Trust You, Father, No Matter What"

Can we call what Danny has "faith"? Many people misunderstand it this way. In actuality, however, that's not what faith is at all. Faith isn't thinking positive thoughts about a situation until you finally convince yourself it will work out the way you want. When the three friends of Daniel were threatened with being thrown into the fiery furnace because they refused to bow down to the idol of King Nebuchadnezzar, their response was one of great faith:

Our God whom we serve is able to deliver us from the furnace of blazing fire; and He will deliver us out of your hand, O king. But even if He does not, let it be known to you, O king, that we are not going to serve your gods or worship the golden image that you have set up (Daniel 3:17-18).

The faith of Shadrach, Meshach, and Abednego was in their God, regardless of what the outcome of their circumstances might be. They said, "Our God is going to deliver us one way or the other. It may be that He delivers us *from* the fire, or He may deliver us *through* the fire, but either way we are going to trust Him." These young men weren't rebuking the flames or affirming aloud that they wouldn't go into the fire. They were simply looking to God and trusting in Him.

The fact is, like many others in the past, Danny could have lost his job. If he had, though, that wouldn't have meant that his faith had failed him or that God had let him down. It would simply have been the way his heavenly Father was working in Danny's life to move him ahead in carrying out the divine plan He has for him.

I'm not suggesting there aren't times when we can believe with confidence that things will turn out the way we are hoping. There are some things that we know without a doubt are God's will because of His Word to us. I'm discussing here the times when we can't be sure what His will is because He has been silent on the matter. At times like that, we can't try to use what we might call "faith" as a way to force God's hand and get Him to do what we want.

To confidently walk in God's will for your life, the only thing you need to do is trust Him. Faith is nothing more and nothing less than looking at things through the lens of confidence in God and His Word.

> Do you feel like you have weak faith? Then remind yourself of who God is and of the fact that He is always reliable.

The answer, then, to feelings of weak faith is simply to focus on the truths we know about our God. Do you feel like you have weak faith? Then remind yourself of who God is and of the fact that He is always reliable. That's true no matter how unstable life seems. You don't have to feel great confidence about what the outcome of your circumstances will be. You only need to throw yourself in total abandon on the One who will determine that outcome and rest in Him, waiting for Him to do what He will do, even though you can't make any sense of it at the time.

So when your faith seems weak, don't worry about it. What else can we expect of ourselves? Thank God, Jesus has enough faith that if we simply cling to Him, everything will work out just fine. Live by *His* faith, remembering that even the faith we call "ours" is a grace-gift of God. The King James translation of Galatians 2:20 helps bring out this truth. Paul says, "The life which I now live in the flesh, I live *by the faith of the Son of God.*" Living by His faith is a lot easier than trying to muster up your own.

Do you get the difference of this approach? As we choose to trust in the faith of Christ, knowing that His faith and ability are sufficient, we are growing in faith, giving glory to God—exactly what Paul said Abraham did. The focal point is Him, not you and the level of your faith.

### Relying on Him Through the Ups and Downs

The psalmist was a man like us. He experienced highs and lows in his spiritual pilgrimage. Let's consider some of the truths revealed to him by the Holy Spirit concerning how God guides us. Again, see how God Himself is the focus.

> You are my rock and my fortress;
>> For Your name's sake You will lead me and guide me.
>>> —Psalm 31:3

> O, send out Your light and Your truth, let them lead me.
>> —43:3

Such is God,
>    Our God forever and ever; He will guide us
>       until death.

—48:14

With Your counsel You will guide me,
>    And afterward receive me to glory.

—73:24

If I ascend to heaven, You are there;
>    If I make my bed in Sheol [Hebrew for "the grave"],
>       behold, You are there.
If I take the wings of the dawn,
>    If I dwell in the remotest part of the sea,
Even there Your hand will lead me,
>    And Your right hand will lay hold of me.

—139:8-10

Consider also what the prophet Isaiah said:

Like a shepherd He will tend His flock,
>    In His arm He will gather the lambs
And carry them in His bosom;
>    He will gently lead the nursing ewes.

—Isaiah 40:11

The LORD will continually guide you,
>    And satisfy your desire in scorched places,
And give strength to your bones;
>    And you will be like a watered garden,
And like a spring of water whose waters do not fail.

—Isaiah 58:11

And here is what Jesus said about the leadership of the Holy Spirit, who lives in us: "When He, the Spirit of truth, comes, He will guide you into all the truth" (John 16:13).

He will guide you into *"all* the truth"! God is trustworthy and has promised to lead us. We have the choice. We can remain unbelieving and afraid, or we can rest in His promises and believe Him. If we want to learn to be led by God, we need to look to the indwelling life of Jesus Christ. He must be our focus.

[To grow in our faith means no more than growing in our knowledge of the indwelling Christ.] We must learn to trust *Christ in us* to guide our steps, to guide our thoughts, and to live His life through us. As Christ lives His life through us, we *will* walk in faith and experience God's will to the fullest extent. Whether it's a wrecked car, like Barry experienced, or the threat of a job loss, like Danny faced, or any other kind of challenge that may come our way, our trust is in the Lord. No matter what happens, He will see to it that we don't fall short of carrying out what He has in mind for our lives.

## God's Will for Us Is Jesus Christ

The will of God is not a complicated matter when we understand the role Jesus Christ has in our lives in regard to God's will for us. We will discover in the following chapters that Jesus not only *shows us* God's will for our lives, but that He *is* God's will for our lives! That distinction will become very important as we move forward. Christ will ensure that we stay within God's will as we increasingly learn to trust in Him. *Christ's life* is our guide to the eternal will of God.

How do we grow in our knowledge of Jesus? That is the role of the Holy Spirit. In the passage I cited above, just after Jesus says that the Holy Spirit will lead us into all the truth, he says that the Holy Spirit "will glorify Me, for He will take of Mine, and He will disclose it to you. All things that the Father has are Mine; therefore I said that He takes of Mine and will disclose it to you" (John 16:14-15).

This is a very important point, theologically and practically. Many sincere believers have gone off on a tangent because they have failed to understand what Jesus was saying here. According to the Lord, what is the message and focus of the Holy Spirit? *The Son, Jesus Christ.* He will show you the plan God has for you as He reveals more and more about the Person who gave Himself for you, then to you.

The Holy Spirit always glorifies the name of Jesus and makes Him known. The Spirit's role in your life is to enable you to know Christ and to empower you to completely depend on Him as He lives His life through you. Don't pray for more faith. You don't need more faith. You already have what you need because you have Jesus. Pray to know Him more intimately. Out of that intimacy, the specifics of His will for you will emerge.

If you want to know the will of God, you need to understand the intimate relationship you have to His Son. The will of God is contained in the Person of Jesus Christ from now throughout eternity to come. He will guide you, not only in this life but in the one to come. He is God's will for us personified. It all revolves around Jesus Christ. [Focus on an external plan and you'll likely find yourself confused and frustrated. Focus on the eternal Son of God and there's no way you'll miss the will of God.]

## Choose to Actively Follow and Learn from Christ

Since all of life and eternity revolve around Jesus, we can begin in this life to walk in the will of God with confidence and boldness. As believers, we have already entered into the eternal. We have been "seated with Christ in the heavenlies." Whatever happens on this side of heaven, we can rest, knowing confidently that it's all going to be okay.

Reality for us is the fact that we are already seated with Christ. That is why we can breathe a sigh of relief about whatever we face. We take comfort in and appropriate the words of Jesus:

> Come to Me, all who are weary and heavy-laden, and I will give you rest. Take My yoke upon you and learn from Me, for I am gentle and humble in heart, and you will find rest for your souls. For My yoke is easy and my burden is light (Matthew 11:28-30).

Christ calls us to become learners, followers, and students—the biblical word is *disciple*. That's what He means by taking on His "yoke." To take on a yoke is to be led, guided, and controlled by Him. He is saying, "I will show you the way."

Jesus Christ is a gentle guide. He isn't a whip-cracking tyrant who grows impatient because you "just don't get it." He is gentle and humble in heart. He loves you and always has your best interests at heart. He can be completely trusted to work out every detail of your life according to the exact specifications the Father has designed for you.

It is time to decide to follow Christ. It is time to irrevocably decide where you will put your trust. Once that decision is made, as problems or challenges come, you don't have to sit around trying to figure out what God's intentions are. You can simply rest in the covenant your God has established for you.

You can rest knowing that He does all things for your good in spite of anything your circumstances may tell you to the contrary. Are you going to believe God? Is He trustworthy? Those are the questions that have to be answered before the bad times come—and they *will* come.

We live in a fallen world. Just as Abraham proved, there will surely be times when we fall into sin, when we don't act like who we are. Instead of allowing Christ to animate our lives, there will be times we decide to momentarily go our own way. That will only lead to foolish decisions and actions. But isn't it wonderful to realize that even though God knows all these things, He still leads us into His will for our lives!

> God is much more interested that you know *who you are* than what you should do.

He will continue to watch over us in all of our foolishness and will walk with us every step of the way. Whether we run well or whether we fall, He is always with us. God will use every event in our lives to serve His purpose. We won't change His plan for our lives by what we do or don't do. He will have the final word. His purpose for our lives continues to move forward—and that purpose is good and loving and perfect!

We are little children, who would never find our way if it were left up to us. But it's not left up to us. Our lives are in the hands of the omnipotent, sovereign God who has created this whole universe and continues to rule and sustain it. He will accomplish His purpose in you and through you.

Stop focusing on all the different options and alternatives you have. Stop worrying and crying out, "What should I do? What should I do?" God is much more interested that you know *who you are* than what you should do.

Focus your attention and devotion on Jesus Christ, trusting Him *to be who He is* through you. When you trust Him to be who He is through you, the will of God becomes apparent. Don't worry that your faith doesn't seem strong to you. Stop evaluating the level of your faith, and simply look at Christ. That's how the plan God has for you will become clear to you.

The apostle Paul wrote in 1 Corinthians 2:16, "Who has known the mind of the Lord, that he will instruct Him? But we have the mind of Christ." Jesus Christ wants to live His life through you. Not only does He want to live His life through you, He wants to *think His thoughts* through you. You don't have to agonize over it. Just abandon yourself and your situation to Him.

## Don't Fleece Yourself

When we fail to trust the indwelling Christ to bring about God's will in our lives, we end up doing other things to try to find God's will. One of those things is widely known as "putting out a fleece." The idea comes from the Old Testament story of Gideon.

In Judges 6, the story is told of how Gideon sought to know God's will. The Lord had called Gideon to deliver Israel from her enemies, but he was afraid. Because of his small stature and physical weakness, he doubted what he had heard God say to him. Maybe he had misunderstood. He wanted to be sure beyond all doubt that God wanted him to be Israel's leader, so he devised a test. Gideon prayed,

> "If You will deliver Israel through me, as You have spoken, behold, I will place a fleece of wool on the threshing floor. If there is dew on the fleece only, and it is dry on all the ground, then I will know that You will deliver Israel through me, as You have spoken." And it was so. When he arose early the next morning and squeezed the fleece, he drained the dew from the fleece, a bowl full of water. Then Gideon said to God, "Do not let Your anger burn against me that I may speak once more; please let me make a test once more with the fleece, let it now be dry only on the fleece, and let there be dew on all the ground." God did so that night; for it was dry only on the fleece, and dew was on all the ground (Judges 6:36-40).

By putting out the fleece before the Lord, Gideon saw God's will affirmed to him. Don't think, however, that the action of Gideon is intended to be an example for you to follow. The Bible makes it clear that when Gideon laid the fleece before the Lord, it was *not* an action of faith; it was actually an expression of *faithlessness* on his part! It was an expression of *doubt* in God's word and fear about his circumstances.

Note again what Gideon says in verse 37: "If there is dew on the fleece only, and it is dry on all the ground, then I will know that You will deliver Israel through me, *as You have spoken.*" Gideon wasn't trying to know God's will with this fleece. God had already spoken, and Gideon admits knowing that. His problem wasn't that he didn't know what to do. His problem was, he doubted whether or not God really meant what He had said. Gideon's fleece was an expression of doubt, not faith!

God had already spoken on this issue. He had already made His will clear to Gideon, but Gideon didn't believe Him. Make no mistake about it. Gideon's use of the fleece was an act of unbelief, an act of doubt. It was not an expression of faith. God, being the God of grace He is, responded to the request. But don't think for a minute that

Gideon's actions should be a template for how we should behave when it comes to knowing God's will.

## You Have the Holy Spirit!

Before we are too hard on Gideon, however, let us remember that, unlike New Testament believers, Gideon did not possess the indwelling Holy Spirit. From our human perspective, he may have had an understandable excuse. We do not. We live in the New Testament, not the Old. This new covenant, of which you are a beneficiary, puts you in a much, much better place than Gideon.

We have Christ, alive and living in us, with His presence and power available to us. And yet, many believers today still say they use a "fleece" to determine God's will. This is not only an expression of unbelief and doubt, but can sometimes be so far removed from biblical faith that is borders on downright superstition.

This may be contrary to what you have believed or heard, but Gideon's story proves my point, and I stand by it. We don't need to use a "fleece" to determine God's will in the New Testament age. We have the Holy Spirit.

When I taught this at a church retreat one weekend, Sharon made a beeline to me after the session had ended. "I'm having a problem with what you said about putting out a fleece," she said. "I've put out fleeces to the Lord many times and He has often made His will clear to me in that way."

"Good, I believe you," I reply. "That just shows that God is a merciful and gracious God, and that He worked *in spite* of your expression of 'faith' as you have understood it in the past. It's very clear in the passage about Gideon that when he put out a fleece, it wasn't faith that caused him to do it. It was doubt."

"So are you saying I shouldn't do that anymore?" Sharon asked.

"What I'm saying is that you have the Holy Spirit living inside you. It isn't necessary for you to look for some sort of external sign to know God's will when, all the while, the eternal Spirit of God is living in you and is ready and able to make God's will known to you."

Although God is amazingly patient and merciful to us in our weakness and ignorance, we need to move beyond this kindergarten method of trying to determine His will. In Christ, God has lifted us to possibilities unimaginably greater! We have the Holy Spirit living inside of us. So why would we not learn to trust *God* instead of trusting in a "fleece"? Because "we have the mind of Christ," we have an advantage Old Testament believers couldn't imagine.

## What You See...or Who You Know?

As God's child, you have divine ability to see life through the eyes of faith, allowing Christ to see and live and work and love through you. You are a conduit of His life into this world. The One who controls it all, lives in and through you. Let that be a truth that stirs your faith.

Don't worry about missing God's will. Go ahead and act in faith, believing that He wants you to grow in this area. The apostle Paul once said, "When I was child, I used to speak like a child, think like a child, reason like a child; when I became a man, I did away with childish things" (1 Corinthians 13:11). There's nothing wrong with being a child, but the idea of *remaining* a child is abnormal. The time has come to act in maturity in regard to discovering and doing God's will in your life. If you'll step out in faith, you'll see that He will faithfully guide you and see to it that you reach the destination He has in mind for you.

> As we begin to see ourselves as God sees us, we are then empowered to live above what our circumstances tell us.

Trusting in His indwelling Spirit is much better than putting out vague "fleeces" that can often be interpreted in any way you choose to interpret them. You are God's child. He loves you and wants to speak to you and teach you to follow His leadership in a spiritually mature way. He wants you to enjoy the benefits of the New Covenant, through which He has promised to never leave or forsake you but to lead you into all truth. It's time to see yourself as His child. A new day has come. It's a day when Christ lives inside you and guides you into the Father's perfect will for your life.

It is of great importance that you learn to identify yourself from the divine perspective. As we begin to see ourselves as God sees us, we are then empowered to live above what our circumstances tell us. Our trust is not in what we see, but in Who we know.

## ❀ G.R.A.C.E. Group Questions ❀

1. At the beginning of this chapter, the story is told of Barry having a car accident after he altered his normal morning routine. Explain your viewpoint on accidents in life. How do you reconcile the fact that God is in charge with the reality that painful events sometimes seem to spontaneously happen in our lives?

2. In Romans 4:20-21, the apostle Paul describes Abraham's great faith—yet we know that Abraham expressed doubts and committed sins many times after God made His covenant with him. In light of this, how would you define the meaning of faith? How do the biblical examples of people with faith differ from contemporary teaching on the subject? What would you say to somebody who suggests you need more faith?

3. What is the meaning of 1 Corinthians 2:16? What does it mean to say that you have the mind of Christ? How would you answer the objection that to say we have Christ's mind is to suggest we think we *are* Jesus Christ?

4. Read the story of Gideon in Judges 6. Where does that story show that putting out a fleece was a sign of his doubt and not his faith? Does God still respond to people who put out a fleece today? Why or why not? What is the New Testament prescription for understanding God's will for our lives? How does John 16:13 address this issue?

5. Explain how the following verses can speak to a person about knowing God's will for his life: Psalm 9:10, Psalm 125:1, Proverbs 3:5, Nahum 1:7, Matthew 6:26-30, Romans 5:2, Romans 10:17, Hebrews 11:1.

# CHAPTER 3

# Be Clear About Who You Are

EVERYWHERE YOU GO, IT'S THE SAME QUESTION. Once somebody knows your name, if they want to know more about you, it's what they ask. Regardless of where they come from, what their socioeconomic level is, how educated they are or aren't, it is *the* thing they want to know about you. "What do you do?" That's it. To most people, your value in this world boils down to your answer to that question. Tell them you're a brain surgeon and you'll rank high with them. Tell them you're the guy who picks up their trash at the curb on Tuesday mornings and you'll likely get a very different response.

We are all born with an irresistible drive to discover a sense of identity. We must find the answer to the question "Who am I?" All our attitudes and actions are driven and colored by our sense of who we are. Sadly, for most people, what they do determines what they think about who they are.

Listen to people introduce themselves, and you will see where they go to determine their sense of self. After giving their names, they will say things like these:

- "I'm a pilot."
- "I'm a basketball player."

47

- "I'm a mechanic."
- "I'm an insurance salesman."
- "I'm Stephen's mother."
- "I'm Mary's husband."
- "I'm the mayor's son."

Practically everybody does it. Society programs us to think of ourselves according to our abilities, our appearance, and our roles in other people's lives. But we create problems for ourselves when we identify ourselves by what we do instead of by who God has created us to be. An important key in knowing God's will for your life is to understand that *who you are* is infinitely more important than anything you may do or not do during your lifetime.

## Are You Stuck in a Lie?

Jesus taught that when we know the truth, it will cause us to become free (see John 8:31-32). If the effect of knowing truth is to set us free, then the opposite is also true: The effect of misunderstandings and believing lies is to put us in bondage.

Vince had been told all his life that the men of his family had always been *real* men, *manly* men. "Stop crying! Only sissies cry! Don't act like a baby!" his dad had repeatedly told him when he was a child. He had been pushed toward being an athlete and a hunter and a fisherman. His older brother had joined the Marines as soon as he was old enough to enlist.

Vince spoke to me one day with a grimace on his hardened yet hollow face. "I know I've been a disappointment," he said. "I never excelled at sports. I didn't want to sign up for military service. I've wanted to become a schoolteacher ever since I became a teenager and was impacted by Mr. Burleson, my eighth-grade teacher."

When Vince announced to his family that he planned to pursue a secondary-education major in college, his dad flipped. "There's no money in that!" he told him in the all-too-familiar condescending manner Vince had grown up seeing.

Vince went to college anyway to pursue his dream, but as he talked to me he expressed doubts about whether or not he was doing the right thing.

"Maybe my dad's right," he said. "Maybe I'm setting my goal too low in life. I don't want to be a loser. Maybe I could do better. But I want to teach. I just wish I knew what God wants me to do. I feel like I'm in the dark on the whole thing."

As we talked together, I could see the agonizing effects his doubts were having on him. He didn't want to take the path his dad had pointed him toward, but he couldn't seem to find peace on the pathway he had chosen. Sadly, many people are like Vince. They don't know what they want, but they question if what they're doing right now is "the right thing."

## Where Your Value Comes From

If you want to confidently discover and do God's will for your life, you absolutely must understand the theme of this chapter. *Who you are is not determined by what you do.* As Christians, a brain surgeon and a garbage collector have the same value, and both can equally fulfill God's plan for their lives.

Your value comes from the fact that you are God's child. That is the essence of who you are. He has created you in His image. In fact, the Bible says you are a work of art, made by Him. Once that truth becomes a reality to you, you will find yourself freed up to do whatever you want to do. You don't have to prove anything to anybody—not to others, not to yourself, and certainly not to God.

Billy Graham preached the gospel to more people in larger gatherings than anybody who has ever lived. Mother Teresa gave her life to help the poor in Calcutta, one person at a time. Whose contribution was greatest? It is a ridiculous question to even ask. They have both fulfilled their mission on Planet Earth.

Once you know who you are, you will be set free to carry out

God's plan for your life, whether it is in obscurity or in the public eye. Vince's problem was that he hadn't become convinced that the career he chose didn't define him. Consequently, he couldn't find peace. Can you relate to his dilemma?

It's a dangerous thing to base your self-perception on what you do, because that can change in a split second. Anything you do to give yourself a sense of who you are is tenuous at best. It can be taken away in the blink of an eye.

> It is essential for us to base what we believe about ourselves on the objective truth of God's Word.

We can lose a job, we can grow older and lose our youthful good looks, and we can lose a relationship through divorce or death. All of these things *will* be taken away eventually, by time if nothing else. It is essential for us to base what we believe about ourselves on the objective truth of God's Word, instead of on the subjective perceptions we have about truth, because that can change from day to day.

No wonder terrible insecurity and fear are so common among human beings. Where can we find a true answer, one that is secure and truly adequate for life? There is only one place: We must discover *who God says we are!* That is, we must learn about and base our self-perception on who God has made us to be in Christ.

## God's New Work of Creation: *You!*

Knowing the truth about who you are will set you free and powerfully change your life. Having become clear about who you are, you'll find that you will be able to relax about what you do because you'll understand that doing flows out of being. Those who don't rest in the assurance of the great value they already possess simply because they are God's child will forever be driven by an internal need to prove something by what they do. That gnawing insecurity will never be satisfied by doing, no matter how much they accomplish. God didn't create us in such a way that the deepest needs of our hearts can ever be completely satisfied by doing. Only He can satisfy our deepest needs for love, value, and acceptance.

Accomplishments cannot fulfill anyone. Do you know what the following people have in common? Ernest Hemingway, Jim Carrey, Hans Christian Anderson, Dick Cavett, Abraham Lincoln, Jean-Claude Van Damme, John Bunyan, and Patty Duke—all of them, despite their achievements, experienced debilitating emotional issues: bipolar diagnosis, depression, anxiety too great to handle.

After conquering the known world, it is said that Alexander the Great wept because there were no more worlds to conquer. Mozart, one of the greatest composers who ever lived, began writing music at the age of five. Ironically, he battled depression almost all of his life because he felt like a failure. In the testimony of her own journey in faith, Mary Kay Ash tells how that after experiencing the success of her Mary Kay Cosmetics empire, "I felt like a complete failure as a woman."

## My Experience with the "Accomplishments Method"

I've seen in my own life experiences the reality of how accomplishments cannot fulfill a person. I served as a senior pastor in local churches for over 20 years. For most of those years I was still in legalism. I believed that fulfilling my destiny was directly connected to my doing an admirable job. In my first book, *Grace Walk,* I wrote about my pilgrimage from a legalistic lifestyle into the grace walk I enjoy today.

The underlying belief with legalism is this: We become what we ought to be by what we *do.* The reality of the matter is just the opposite. It's when we discover who we are that we become empowered to rise up and fulfill God's will for our lives. But for years I didn't know that. So I struggled to be a successful pastor, as measured by an expanding ministry and public affirmation. Like many people, I thought I had to do to *be.*

The thing that was a mystery for me during those years was, no matter how great the external signs of success, deep inside I always felt like something was missing. In fact, I felt hypocritical despite the fact I was doing my best. I often felt like a personal failure...even at times I knew I was considered a public success.

I recall one phase in my life that might be considered the peak of my pastoral ministry. I served in a loving congregation where most of the people adored me. They would often express their love through their words. They also showered me with thoughtful expressions of affirmation through their actions. When I wanted to pursue my doctoral degree, they paid for it in advance. When I suggested I wanted to go on a mission trip, they gave me the necessary funds for it. It was pretty much the case that, if they knew I really wanted something, it happened. They were extremely accommodating and encouraging. Through their words and actions, they gave me every reason to believe that life could get no better.

The church was the fastest-growing one in the county, which only served to strengthen my legalistic idea that God's blessings on a church can always be measured by numbers. I was well respected in our town, as evidenced by receiving the "Outstanding Young Religious Leader" award from a local civic club one year. In every measurable way, it seemed to me that things were on the move, upward and onward.

### Faster, Higher, Stronger?

In the midst of it all, however, I experienced an internal restlessness. To me, it seemed like the church was growing but I wasn't. Everybody loved me except me. I was hard on myself. In order to fulfill God's will for my life, I had to be a certain way. I needed to improve myself. I tried to do that through the disciplines prescribed to me from the days of my childhood—read the Bible more, pray more, evangelize more, give more, witness more, and so on.

The key to the whole issue of doing God's will (so I thought) revolved around me doing more and more things in a better and better way. Though I was successful outwardly, I felt like I was a failure inwardly. Only years later did the Lord show me that His will for my life didn't revolve around what I could do for Him. Instead, His will for my life was, first and foremost, that I would come to know who I am based on my relationship to Him. I would come to learn that what I do in no way defines me. God's specific plan for each of our lives rests on the understanding He wants us to have of who we *are*. And that understanding is rooted in what *He has already done* on our behalf through Christ.

The point here is, whether a person has a glamorous career like that of an actor, a powerful position like that of a president, a religious role like that of a pastor, or any other place others might consider successful, it is still possible to feel like a failure. *What we do* can never "scratch the itch" to feel fulfilled. So we might as well not go there to find what we're looking for in life.

It's not that what you do in life isn't important—it is. Rather, there is only one way we can be free *to do* with a healthy attitude. That's when we aren't trying to milk life out of our accomplishments, because we know our life is grounded in Christ and nothing else. Once we know that, we find ourselves free to pursue the things we choose to do in life with confident expectancy, knowing the outcome doesn't reflect who we are. We can move full speed ahead, joyfully knowing that we are pursuing the vision God has put in our hearts—and joyfully knowing that, win or lose, we're still winners because what we do doesn't define us. Our Creator has already done that.

## Know Who You Are, Then Do What You Do

Once you know who you are, then you can do what you do with divine optimism. Can you imagine the difference it would make in your level of confidence about the life path you choose if you really believe that Christ is placing the desires within you that are there and has committed Himself to see they are fulfilled? That isn't an I-only-wish-it-were-so scenario. When you know who you are, you understand that's literally the way it is.

All believers have some understanding about who they are. To varying degrees, they know something of the benefits Christ has purchased for us through His death and resurrection. Unfortunately, many don't seem to understand much beyond forgiveness of sins and going to heaven when they die. As wonderful as those truths are, they are only the beginning.

For one thing, becoming a Christian is not only about getting something we didn't have before (such as forgiveness); it is about *becoming* someone we were not before! "If anyone is in Christ, he is a new creature; the old things passed away; behold, new things have come" (2 Corinthians 5:17). God made something new when He made you. You're a one-of-a-kind creation. That fact is huge.

### What Does "New Creation" Mean?

It's amazing to consider. The opening chapter of the Bible, Genesis 1, tells how God created everything in six days. Then He rested, but not because He was tired. It was because He was *finished*. Modern science agrees with this. The law of conservation of matter and energy states that nothing new is being created in the universe. Since God finished His work in the beginning, there have been only two exceptions to this—only two new things God has created:

**1. God did an act of new creation when He raised Jesus from the dead.** Jesus' resurrection wasn't just a "resuscitation," a reviving of His original human body. God raised His Son as the first Man inhabiting an eternal, immortal, glorified body, the kind we will share in eternity. His resurrected body was the first of a new order instituted by God, anticipating the day when He will make "new heavens and a new earth" (2 Peter 3:13). That's why Paul calls Christ "the first fruits" from the dead (1 Corinthians 15:20). He is the "first edition" of an entirely new kind of man—yet only the first of a great harvest still to come.

**2. God performed a new act of creation when He saved you.** As Paul says, "if anyone is in Christ, he is a new creature." In other words, when you put your faith in Christ, God made something brand-new. He created you as someone who literally belongs to a new species. You are in union with His Seed—Jesus Christ.

Similar to His description of Jesus, your new life is described as "the first fruits of the Spirit" (Romans 8:23) because it is only the first installment of what He plans to do with you. One day God will give you a new immortal body to go with your new identity. While you live here on earth, in the in-between stage, He has some great plans for you. Knowing what He has done in us to equip us for this interim time on Planet Earth will excite your imagination about your God-given potential.

> The resurrection of Christ was God's solution to man's state of spiritual death, providing life in a new act of creation.

Let's start with the problem Christ has solved for us. In God's sight, the problem with the fall of man is far more drastic than many people realize. Man didn't just need rehabilitation. We needed resurrection. Apart from Christ, we were sinners, guilty before a holy God and in need of forgiveness. That's certain, but it wasn't the worst part of our condition. We were actually spiritually dead and in need of life! We weren't just sin-sick. We were as dead as dead can get. Paul said in Ephesians 2:1 that we were dead in our trespasses and sins.

The solution for guilt is forgiveness, and the solution for death is life. That is exactly what God has provided for us through Jesus Christ. We have been given both forgiveness and life.

> God, being rich in mercy, because of His great love with which He loved us, even when we were dead in our transgressions, made us alive together with Christ (by grace you have been saved), and raised us up with Him, and seated us with Him in the heavenly places in Christ Jesus (Ephesians 2:4-6).

To fully understand the gospel, we must grasp both parts of God's work. The death of Jesus Christ on the cross was God's solution to man's problem of sin and guilt, providing forgiveness and acceptance.

The resurrection of Christ was God's solution to man's state of spiritual death, providing life in a new act of creation.

### God Created You for a Purpose

Having made us alive in Christ, God the Father gave us a divine destiny. What purpose does He have in mind for those who have received all this in Christ? The Bible tells us that "we are His workmanship, created in Christ Jesus for good works, which God prepared beforehand so that we would walk in them" (Ephesians 2:10). Now we are getting to the subject at hand—what He has in mind for you *now*.

The Greek word translated "workmanship" is *poema*, the same word from which we get our English word *poem*. It means a masterfully crafted object, like a piece of poetry, a painting, or a sculpture. In other words, you are God's work of art!

You have been "created in Christ Jesus" with a divine purpose in mind—to glorify God by participating in His works in this world. That's where the will of God intersects with your identity. His plan for you is to express Him through your day-to-day activities in a way that is uniquely you.

You have much good to offer the world. You don't work *for* God, but rather join together *with* God as a co-laborer together with Him. The good works of your life aren't your gifts to God. They are actually His gifts to you, prepared for you before you were even born.

You can know for sure that one aspect of God's will for your life is this: that you enjoy sharing with Him in expressions of His love toward this world, manifested through the good works He has prepared and empowered you to do. That's a far cry from the legalistic approach many of us have believed. We don't *have to* do good works. We *get to* do them because of our Father's generosity!

Those "good works" don't always appear to be spectacular. But then they don't have to be. A monk named Brother Lawrence wrote a book, centuries ago, that still inspires believers today, called *Practicing the Presence of God*. He writes of walking in awareness of God's presence while doing the most ordinary things of daily life. He wrote, "I can scrub out a kitchen pot to the glory of God."

The same is true for you and me. We can do laundry, go to work, raise children, pay our bills, and even enjoy rest and recreation to the glory of God. Whatever we do can be offered to God through a heart of faith, and He will receive it as worship. And how much His name is honored when we do acts of love, kindness, mercy, and generosity in the name of Christ!

### Relax—You Don't Have to Look Religious

As far as your outward actions in this world are concerned, you have been created *for* something—good works—or to be more precise, *God's* works that He does through you. But again, don't think for one minute that the works He has planned for you have to look religious. Whether you practice medicine or law, whether you drive a truck or serve tables in a restaurant, whether you are a homemaker or a contractor, whatever you do in life is God at work in and through you to express Himself. Don't think for an instant that what you are doing with your life isn't as spiritual as what somebody else might be doing. As Christ lives through you, *everything you do is spiritual.* Not religious, maybe, but most definitely spiritual.

Kate is a special-education teacher at an elementary school. One day after listening to an audio teaching I did on this subject, she sent me the following e-mail:

> Thank you for helping me to understand the spiritual nature of what I'm doing with my life. When I was a young girl, I thought God was calling me to be a missionary. When I went to college, it was my intention to prepare for a life on "a foreign mission field." What I didn't expect was to almost immediately meet somebody there who would become my husband. He believed that his calling in life was to practice law. His dream of being a lawyer and mine of being a foreign missionary didn't match up.

I loved Jim and so we were married. I have had a happy marriage all these years and have loved the Lord, but deep down I've felt like I may have compromised in what I believed God had shown me to do. Today, as I listened to your teaching about how Christ lives through us at every moment, I got it. I *am* a missionary! I bring the love of Jesus Christ to a group of children every day and help them to see how much He really loves them. I finally get it—that what I am doing here is no less spiritual than if I were teaching the Bible on a foreign mission field to people who had never heard the name of Christ.

I was so happy over Kate's realization. God's will for our lives is that Christ expresses Himself through us wherever we find ourselves in life. What we do may not look religious, but that doesn't matter at all. What is important is that what we do is spiritual because the Spirit of Christ is doing it through us.

We can live a life of peace, contentment, and quiet confidence when we begin to understand our identity in Christ—and live comfortably out of that identity. How different it is from the spirit of bondage that comes from legalism! God's will for you is that you know who you are, relax, and simply act like it in your daily routine. That's an offer that will cause you to experience the kind of rest Jesus promised! (see Matthew 11:28-30).

## Grasping What Your Riches in Christ Are

The New Testament teaches many truths about a believer's identity in Christ. It is mind-boggling to discover how great God's goodness is to us in Him! When we begin to grasp these truths, their impact will change not only our thinking about ourselves, but the way we live our lives and the decisions we make. We live out of the confidence of knowing this—however God sees us to be is exactly who we are. With that in mind, consider a few things the Bible says about what God has given you through Christ:

**You have been given eternal life.** "The wages of sin is death, but the free gift of God is eternal life in Christ Jesus our Lord" (Romans 6:23). Eternal life is more than a home in heaven. It is Jesus Christ Himself. You have been joined in union with Deity—Jesus Christ! Armed with that knowledge, you can charge forward into life knowing that you possess a supernatural ability that uniquely equips you for your life calling.

**You have been forgiven.** "In Him we have redemption through His blood, the forgiveness of our trespasses, according to the riches of His grace which He lavished on us" (Ephesians 1:7-8). Jesus absorbed every sin of your lifetime into Himself on the cross. He paid for every sin you would ever commit, though at the time you hadn't been born to commit even one of them. Now, in Him, you have been given forgiveness for every last one of them!

A clear conscience is a valuable asset when it comes to being productive in life. Gnawing guilt is a drag on forward progress, but a conscience free from regrets and guilt empowers us to live in carefree abandon as we pursue our God-given goals. You don't have to look backward in regret. Instead, you can always look forward with optimistic anticipation.

**You have been justified—declared totally righteous, not guilty.** "Having been justified by faith, we have peace with God through our Lord Jesus Christ" (Romans 5:1). We don't ever have to be afraid that God looks at us in a negative way at all, because He has removed all the negatives from us by Christ's finished work on the cross. It has been said that "justify" means it is just-as-if-I never sinned! You don't just have a clean future, you have a clean past!

> Knowing who you are changes everything!

God is on your side. He isn't going to bless you in spite of yourself. He is going to bless you because He is *for* you. Realizing that fact will embolden you in everything you do. You'll find yourself acting in confidence because you know God is for you.

**You are a saint—a holy one.** When Paul wrote to the church in Corinth, he addressed them as "those who have been sanctified in Christ Jesus, saints by calling" (1 Corinthians 1:2). To be "sanctified" or to become a "saint" means that God has *set you apart* as special. He sees you as His beloved possession for His exclusive use. Notice that Paul calls the Corinthian church "saints," even though he wrote two of his longest letters trying to correct problems in their attitudes and behavior. "Saint" is a description of their *identity,* not their actions.

And the same is true of you. Knowing who you are changes everything! You are then equipped to act out of your true identity instead of your feelings. Feelings can deceive you, but when you realize you have been set apart for a divine purpose, you can gradually bring negative feelings into alignment with the truth of God's Word—that you are special and blessed.

**You have become a child of God.** There are two ways you can become someone's child on earth: by birth or by adoption. The Bible teaches that we have become God's children in *both* of those ways. First, we who believe have been "born again" to new life through the agency of the Holy Spirit (see John 3:3-8). The theological word is *regeneration.* We were literally born into the family of God when He gave us His life. Second, we have been adopted as children of God:

> You have not received a spirit of slavery leading to fear again,
> but you have received a spirit of adoption as sons by which
> we cry out, "Abba! Father!" The Spirit Himself testifies with
> our spirit that we are children of God (Romans 8:15-16).

**You are indwelt by the Holy Spirit.** God has not just forgiven us and left us alone to slug it out for the rest of our lives. He has come to live within us in the Person of the Holy Spirit. Another way to say it is that we have *Christ's empowering presence* in us. It's for that reason Paul could say,

> I have been crucified with Christ; and it is no longer I who
> live, but Christ lives in me; and the life which I now live

in the flesh I live by faith in the Son of God, who loved me
and gave Himself up for me (Galatians 2:20).

That's why we can live with resources greater than our own; we have
Christ Himself and His resources living within us. What an edge in
life when it comes to accomplishing your God-given goals!

As I said previously, becoming a Christian is much more than just
having your sins forgiven and going to heaven when you die. As great
as those are, there is much more. As Major Ian Thomas said, the whole
gospel can be summed up in this sentence: "Jesus Christ gave His life
*for* you, so that He could give His life *to* you, so that He could live
His life *through* you." When you understand this, you have grasped
the complete picture.

In a world where so much unhealthy human activity is motivated
by people's drive to establish their identities, we can know for certain
who we are. We can say, "I am a child of God through faith in Jesus
Christ!" Nothing in all creation can change this identity. Circumstances may change. We can lose a job or wealth. We can lose a spouse
or parents. We can even lose our earthly lives. But nothing can change
*who we are.* That is true security! *That* is enough to motivate us to
charge forward toward the goal of carrying out the divine plan for our
lives with confident optimism.

## Living Out Your New Identity

Can you see how a biblical understanding of who you are will free
you up to live at a higher level than you would otherwise experience?
How could the understanding that you are possessed by divine life
*not* make a difference in how you move ahead toward fulfilling God's
will?

It is on the basis of this new identity that the New Testament calls
us to action. One of the most concise examples of how we are urged to
live is found in Ephesians 5:8: "You were formerly darkness, but now
you are Light in the Lord; walk as children of Light."

The sequence in this verse is critically important. Notice what it does *not* say: "You children of darkness—start acting like children of Light so that you can become Light." Rather, it begins with what God has done. He has already changed our identities from darkness to Light in Christ; now He calls us to recognize it and be who He made us to be.

Remember Vince, who against his dad's wishes started college to pursue a teaching career? He said to me, "I feel like I'm in the dark on the whole thing." In time, Vince came to see a life-changing truth that is tied directly to this verse. Although he felt like he was in the dark, he really wasn't. Sometimes our subjective feelings can contradict the objective truth of God's Word. The truth is that you *are* in the Light. Every Christian is in the Light at every moment because, through Jesus Christ, we are continuously in God. "God *is* light and in Him is no darkness at all," the apostle John wrote in 1 John 1:5.

Think about the following statements in terms of their logic:

1. God is always Light and can never contain darkness.

2. As His child, you are always in God.

3. Therefore, you can never be in the darkness.

"But what about when I'm completely confused? Am I not in the darkness then?" someone like Vince might ask. Even then we aren't in the dark, because we are in God. And He is never in the darkness nor is darkness in Him because, by nature, He *is* Light. "What if I sin?" somebody else might protest. "Surely I would be in the darkness then!"

The biblical teaching is that we used to be darkness, but now we are Light in the Lord. We may not always be able to see the light in a situation; we may even willfully blindfold ourselves by sinning, but that doesn't change the fact that we're in the Light. A man wearing a blindfold over his eyes may not see light even when he is standing under a bright floodlight, but that doesn't change the reality that he is still in the light.

Even when we don't understand what to do, God is faithfully leading us toward His will for our lives. In the first nine verses of the twenty-third chapter of the book of Job, this battered saint goes into great detail describing his frustration in attempting to make sense out of God's will as it was unfolding in his life. "I wish I could find God so that I could get some answers," he says (see verses 3-4). "But I can't find Him anywhere I look. It seems like He has disappeared at the time when I need Him most!" (see verses 8-9). Job was blind to the light of the situation, but he affirms his faith in God in verses 10-11: "But He knows the way I take; when He has tried me, I shall come forth as gold. My foot has held fast to His path."

The evidence of Job's faith is seen in the fact that his actions weren't swayed by his emotions. "My foot has held fast to His path" is what Job said he had done, even though feeling at the same time like God had checked out and gone home without him.

As with Job, knowing who God is, then knowing who we are, is what empowers us to move forward in faith—faith that His plan is unfolding even when that doesn't seem to be the case.

When instructing people how to behave, the apostle Paul seemed to use that very same template every time. It has often been suggested that the first part of his epistles is usually doctrinal and the latter part is practical. To understand that in light of our discussion, we might say that Paul begins by laying out the foundation of the believer's identity and then, having established that fact, he goes on to talk about how we are to act.

When you know who you are, it's going to change the way you behave. Do you want to know and do God's will for your life? Then you must be clear about who you are.

Don't think that I've thrown in a theological chapter in the middle of other practical chapters about knowing God's will. This is as practical as it gets. Until we know who we are, we will never be able to confidently do what we've been created to do. However, once we know that we are somebody who is empowered with divine life; that we are a child of God and that He is on our side; that we have been set apart by Him to express His divine life through the unique and specific plan He has for us; then we are then ready to tackle the world.

## ❋ G. R. A. C. E. Group Questions ❋

1. Give a short description of who you are. Is this the person you have always seen yourself to be? If not, how has your understanding of your own identity changed? Why is the issue of having a biblical understanding of our identity so important when it comes to walking in God's will for our lives?

2. Name a few people in modern culture who have experienced great success in their public lives, but whose personal lives have been sources of pain to them. What would you say to these people if you had the opportunity to talk to them? Describe a time in your own life when you felt like a failure despite the fact that things were going well in your circumstances. How did you move beyond that place?

3. Ephesians 2:4-6 powerfully describes what God has done for us through Jesus Christ. How do the things described in these verses apply to the matter of knowing and fulfilling the things God has planned for you in this life?

4. Name somebody in the Bible who wasn't well known, but was mightily used by God. Discuss the following statement made in this chapter: "We can do laundry, go to work, raise children, pay our bills, and even enjoy rest and recreation to the glory of God." Read Colossians 3:17 and then paraphrase the verse in your own words.

5. What are the top three adjectives you would use to describe yourself? What lies have you believed about yourself in the past that you have now rejected? How does a faulty understanding of who we are interfere with our ability to successfully and confidently fulfill God's plan for our lives? What answer does Matthew 9:29 provide to that question?

### ❧ CHAPTER 4

# Trust Your Thoughts

I HOPE THAT AS YOU ARE READING you are finding yourself being encouraged by seeing the great possibilities before you as a child of God. Christ lives in you! What a powerful statement. Is the Holy Spirit energizing your hopes and imagination as you read? I hope so, because it is by knowing who you are that you will be moved forward into the confidence to boldly pursue God's will for your life. Now you can learn to live according to His resources, and not just your own.

It gets even better, though. Not only can we live confident of His life within us and His great love for us, we can move into the knowledge that we also possess the very mind of Christ. This knowledge becomes the springboard from which we come to know and do the will of God. The apostle Paul said, "Who has known the mind of the Lord, that he will instruct him? But we have the mind of Christ" (1 Corinthians 2:16).

The first phrase in that verse is from Isaiah 40:14 in the Old Testament. Consider it: "Who has known the mind of the Lord?" If we look back and compare Isaiah's question with Paul's, we notice a great difference in the context. When Isaiah asked the question, the expected answer was "Nobody! Nobody can know the mind of God." But in the New Testament, under the New Covenant in this time of grace, the answer is completely different. Paul points us to the fact that now every Christian can know the mind of God, because by the life of the indwelling Christ we *have* the mind of God.

### Think About Your Thoughts

"Are you saying that my thoughts are God's thoughts?" Keith asked me after hearing me speak on the subject. "No," I answered, "I'm saying that His thoughts are your thoughts. He will actually put thoughts into your mind that can guide you as you seek to know His will."

> You can trust that, just as Jesus wants to live through you, He wants to *think* through you too.

I've met very few believers who deny the possibility that the enemy of our souls can introduce thoughts into our minds. Haven't all of us experienced times when suddenly, out of nowhere (or so it seems), a terribly sinful thought rushes into our consciousness? I've even had it happen while in prayer. Until I knew better, I used to interrupt whatever I had been praying about and immediately begin to beg "Forgive me, Lord! I can't believe I would think such a thing, especially while I'm praying!"

In time, I came to learn a very important lesson: *Not every thought you have is your own.* Thoughts can be introduced into your mind. As we become grounded in the truth that we were given the righteous nature of Jesus Christ at salvation (see 2 Peter 1:3-4), we are able to learn that Christ can guide us by means of our thought life. In other words, you can trust that, just as Jesus wants to live through you, He wants to *think* through you too.

It *is* therefore possible for us to *know* God's mind concerning His will for our lives—absolutely. How can we? It sounds easy in concept, but if we're being honest, we will all admit that things sometimes don't seem all that clear in our minds. We have a mix of good and bad thoughts, true and faulty beliefs, and admirable and ugly desires. The key is understanding which thoughts are from Him.

Here's the good news: God has given us His Holy Spirit to indwell us, and also several avenues of guidance to discern His mind, so that we can arrive at a knowledge of His will with confidence.

## Five Factors for Grace-Based Decision Making

How can we know that our thoughts are indeed an expression of the mind of Christ? In this chapter, I want to set forth five factors that will give you confidence in the Christ who thinks through you as you face decisions to be made. It is important to understand two things as we consider these five factors.

First, I have chosen the word *factors* carefully. There is an inherent threat to a clear understanding of grace any time a list that describes behavioral choices is given. The tendency is to take that list and turn it into an equation we can count on to get us where we want to be. That is not what these five factors are. They are intended to be more *descriptive* than prescriptive. To put it a different way: These five items tell more about *what will happen* to confirm Christ's thoughts within you than *what you need to do* to have the mind of Christ. Though these five factors aren't a magic formula for knowing God's will, they do seem to be present in the attitude of all Christians who are confident that the thoughts they're having are coming from Him.

To emphasize this point again, I'll say it this way: This is not a mechanical set of "steps" for learning God's will for you. God is a Person who wants a relationship with us, not a computer to be manipulated. Therefore, He doesn't merely give us steps to do. He is a Person to trust, not a formula to figure out. He walks with us and guides us into His will. So think of these five factors as ways He guides you.

Secondly, it is important to emphasize that the New Testament method of decision making is *grace-based,* not legalistic. A legalistic approach is completely different from one that's grace-based. Legalism says, "You've got to go out and *find* the will of God," as if it were some kind of Easter egg hidden in a cosmic field. Further, the burden is on *you* to find the will of God, no matter how obscure it is. (And you sometimes feel like God apparently doesn't care very much whether you succeed or not.) Then, having found His will, it's up to you to do it in your own strength, according to your own abilities.

If you live with this perspective, huge ramifications depend on you finding and doing the right thing. As I commented at the beginning of this book, people who live this way often experience anxiety, frustration, and fear—and it's no wonder they do. That is *not* a grace walk toward understanding God's will. That is *not* the way a loving heavenly Father guides His children. That is *not* what the Bible teaches about how we, as New Testament believers, are to know and experience the mind of God and do His will.

Instead, the five factors I will explain here will describe what the Holy Spirit will do in you so you can confidently know and do the will of God. They all revolve around thinking the thoughts of God, based on the promise of His Word that "we have the mind of Christ."

## Factor #1: We Know God's Will by Resting in Christ

What does it mean to rest in Christ? It is not a spooky, mystical experience that only a few super-Christians can have. It is simply living in the reality of the teaching of the Lord Jesus Himself:

> I am the vine, you are the branches; he who abides in Me and I in him, he bears much fruit; for apart from Me you can do nothing (John 15:5).

The Lord compares our relationship to Him to that of a branch and a vine. Think about the branch for a moment. Does a branch *produce* fruit, or does it *bear* fruit? It's obvious, isn't it? *Produce* is not the right word, because if you detach that branch from the vine, there will be no fruit. A branch has no power in and of itself to produce fruit, but it can *bear* fruit—in fact, that's exactly what it exists for! It is made to live in a dependent relationship where, as it remains attached to and freely receives the life of the vine, fruit will result, visibly attached to the branch.

What do you learn about the Christian life from this? In exactly the same way a branch is dependent on the vine, we are dependent on Christ. Apart from dependence on Him, we "can do nothing," as He says. But, depending on Him and receiving His life, we can bear the fruit of Christ's indwelling life so that it is visible to others.

To be sure, there is a sense in which every Christian abides in Christ. We live eternally in Him, and He lives eternally in us. It is a divine union that will never end. In contrast, in John 15, Jesus uses the word *abide* to show us something about the meaning of dependence on Him alone as our life-source in this world. In that use of the word, it means that we acknowledge Him in all of our ways; that we commit everything in our daily lives to Him; that we act, relying on Him for His ability and on Him for the results; and that we depend on Him to act in and through every detail of our existence as He works out His purpose for our lives. To have the mind of Christ is to trust God to be who He is, in us and through us, as we interpret life through the lens of His indwelling life.

## Resting and Trusting Go Together

God is sovereign, the Creator and Sustainer of the universe. Remember? Somebody bigger than us is in charge of the universe and everything in it. And you are in it. Abiding in Christ means simply that we are at rest internally as we depend on that One who is in charge. Our disposition, then, is "Lord, I am trusting You to guide my thoughts, to stimulate and activate my desires—I am resting in Your ability and intent to orchestrate the events in my life, to make Your will clear to me. I am trusting You as I step out in faith, and I trust You with the results."

The Old Testament gives us glimpses of the grace to come through Jesus Christ, as it relates God's desire to make His will known in our lives. "Commit your works to the LORD and your plans will be established" (Proverbs 16:3); "In all your ways acknowledge Him, and He will make your paths straight" (Proverbs 3:6).

Resting in Christ is a mind-set. It is an attitude toward the Lord, an attitude of complete trust. Abiding in Christ is not some kind of constant verbal reassurance to Him that we trust Him. It doesn't mean I'm going through my day saying, "Lord, I'm trusting you, I'm trusting you, I'm trusting you..." It doesn't even necessarily require that we express it verbally at all. It doesn't necessarily even mean *consciously*—as if every moment we are aware that we are abiding in Him, thinking to ourselves, *I'm abiding, I'm abiding, I'm abiding...*Nor is it by praying a certain number of prayers that we are trusting in Him. No amount of jumping through religious hoops will manipulate God into orchestrating events so they'll go well for us.

As I discussed in an earlier chapter, resting in Christ does not mean simply that we think positively. I've met people who claim to have faith, but something doesn't seem right about their perspective. "I believe!" they boldly say. "*What* do you believe?" I ask. It seems to me sometimes as if their faith is in faith.

Abiding in Christ is more than that. After all, even the world advocates positive thinking. I'm all for positive thinking, but beneath the positive thinking of the Christian there must be a solid *reason* for those positive thoughts. Faith is a *substance,* according to Hebrews 11:1, and that substance rests on something solid. That solid reason is the sovereign God who is our very life in the Person of Jesus Christ.

Resting in Christ means that we have surrendered the deed to our lives into His hands, so that like the apostle Paul, we can say, "It is no longer I who live, but Christ lives in me; and the life which I now live in the flesh I live by faith in the Son of God, who loved me and gave Himself up for me" (Galatians 2:20).

To rest in Christ is to trust Him. It means believing that He is our life, and that He will think His thoughts through us. To experience the will of God as a believer, we will calmly rest in the sufficiency of Jesus Christ. You will know that He is your life; you will trust totally in Him that He will cause you to *know* what His will for your life is. He will cause you to have a *desire* to do His will, and He will *equip* you with the ability to do it. It is depending totally on Him.

## What Happens When You Hand Over Control

Maybe you bought this book because you are facing a specific situation right now where you need to understand His mind. You *want* to know God's will and, once you know it, you are willing to do it.

That's a great place to be. There is one question I want to ask you to consider as you move forward: Have you yielded your life totally into His hands? Are you willing for Him to have His way in the particular situation you face right now, regardless of how it turns out? Have you released the right to have any control over the affairs of your life, and have you acknowledged that you are trusting Him to direct you in the decisions you make and empower you as you move toward carrying out those decisions?

This is bigger than many people realize. The nature of the flesh is to be in control. Its default setting is to do our best to work things out in the way we believe will lead to the best possible outcome. The problem is, with our finite, human insight, we have limited vision. Consequently, our efforts to control a situation are an attempt to perfectly manage something we can't possibly perfectly understand.

To add to the problem, in our attempt to control our circumstances we are often actually fighting *against* the unfolding of our Father's plan for us. It's not that we *want* to do that. It's just that it's so *hard* to let go at times! Letting go is not the default setting of the flesh, that's for sure. And the flesh can seem terribly strong at times.

As Mark and and his wife, Lee, began to understand the biblical truth about letting go, they recalled a scenario they had faced in their own lives: "When we knew the Lord was leading us to move to another city, we bought a new home there and put our old house on the market. Little did we know what a struggle we would have over the house we wanted to sell. For two years, the house was on the market, but nobody wanted it. We knew the Lord had led us to go but couldn't understand why our house back home wouldn't sell. It was about to drive us crazy."

The couple had lowered the price on their home repeatedly. Mark put an advertisement in the newspaper, offering a lease-purchase option to any qualifying tenants who would rent the house and relieve him of the monthly mortgage payment. The real-estate agent, who was Lee's friend, had tried to entice potential buyers with offers of creative financing. No matter what they did to try to sell the house, nothing worked.

## The Relief of Letting Go

One day Mark was praying about it. "Lord," he said, "I know you can do anything. You're the one who created everything and who controls everything. You could sell that house if you *would!*" Later he described that moment this way: "After I reminded the Lord He *could* sell the house if He *would,* the silence was deafening. It was as if, by His silence, God was saying, 'Yes, I could.'

"So I responded, 'It's like...you don't *want* me to sell this house?' Again, the silence seemed like He was saying,

> They decided to give up their attempt to control the situation and just trust God, even though their feelings didn't always say "Amen" to their trust.

'Now you're starting to understand.' 'How am I supposed to make the payment on this house?' I demanded. For the first time during this verbal assault on my Father, words came to my mind that I knew were His voice: 'Which monthly payment have *I* not made yet?'

"I got it. God wanted me to keep our house."

Mark told Lee what had happened when he had prayed. They decided to give up their attempt to control the situation and just trust God, even though their feelings didn't always say "Amen" to their trust.

How did it end? They kept the house and plan to move back into it later in life when they want to be nearer to their family. Meanwhile, God makes the payments, and they still have the house. Their burden became a blessing when they learned to stop trying to control the situation and to simply trust their Father.

None of us easily give up control over our own life circumstances, but when we do, we take great strides toward finding and fulfilling our Father's plan for us. Are you willing to adopt this attitude of complete surrender to Him, forfeiting the deed to everything in your life and putting it into the hands of God?

Such an attitude will suggest a response like this: "Lord, You know me. If You leave it completely up to me and I rely on myself, I'm going to try to make things happen the way I think they should. I acknowledge that I'm not the one who can make that call. Apart from You, I can do nothing! So I'm not going to trust in myself. I am trusting in You. I am abiding in You, depending on You to make Your will clear to me. I'm letting it all go, and I will trust You." This is resting in Christ. It will be the first thing you see happening in you as the Holy Spirit prepares you to discern the mind of God concerning your own circumstances.

## Factor #2: We Know God's Will Is in Agreement with His Word

As we move forward in expressing God's will through our lives, we will see that His will never contradicts the clear teaching of the Bible. This means our thoughts won't be in opposition to what the Bible says—because God doesn't contradict Himself. This is a kindergarten level of understanding, but it is fundamental and needs to be said. Every Christian should understand that God would never lead His children to make decisions contrary to what He has said in His Word.

You may say, "I'm trusting in the Lord, and I feel He's guiding me to do this or that…" Wonderful! You may feel desires and think that it's God, but—does your desire align itself with God's Word? Or is it contrary to what the Scripture says? When God leads you, it will *never* be out of line with the Word. "Your word is a lamp to my feet and a light to my path" (Psalm 119:105). The light of the Word and the leadership of the Spirit will always be in synch. As the thoughts of Christ enter your mind, they will be consistent with the Scripture.

After hearing me teach on this subject one day, Collin came up to me and said, "You know, I saw the truth of this in my own life recently. I was offered a promotion at my company. On the surface, it looked very attractive. Upon closer investigation, though, I learned that a part of my responsibility would require me to mislead our clients. I knew that as a Christian I couldn't do that. I didn't *want* to do that. So I stayed where I am."

Collin is a man who understands how God's will and God's Word line up. He didn't have to think twice about what to do. He understood that God's will always leads us to live the Christ-life. When you are resting in Christ, you can trust your own thoughts—but it is always good to test those thoughts to see if they are in alignment with, or contradictory to, the Word of God.

A woman who was a friend and a church member came to see me one time. She told me, "I've been involved with another man." She was married, and the man was married to another woman. "My husband hasn't walked with the Lord," she continued, "and I've been praying for years that the Lord would give me a good Christian man."

She went on to explain that the man she was involved with was "a good Christian man." Then came the conclusion. "We have decided that the Lord is telling us to divorce our mates and marry each other. So I just wanted to share it with you and get your blessing." I think she would have gone on to ask me if I would perform their wedding ceremony if I hadn't cut her off when I did.

She didn't like my response, because I felt compelled to tell her without hesitation that the choice she was making was *not* the will of God for her life. She became indignant and said she was insulted I would say such a thing. "I *know* this is the will of God," she insisted. I asked how she knew. "I feel it. The Lord just keeps confirming it to me in so many ways."

I had known this woman for many years and felt the freedom to explain to her the same thing I'm sharing with you: The will of God *never* contradicts the Word of God. So when you are seeking to know the appropriate decision you should make, rest in Christ and trust the mind of Christ in you—but always test your thinking according to the Scriptures, knowing that the mind of Christ is always in perfect agreement with God's Word. He will never lead you any other direction. *Rest, but test.* That's a good rule of thumb to follow.

## Factor #3: Mature Christians Often Affirm God's Will

Proverbs 11:14 says, "Where there is no guidance the people fall, but in abundance of counselors there is victory." To regularly make major decisions without seeking counsel from godly, mature believers isn't a pathway I'm comfortable traveling. Speaking in general, you'll never be acting unwisely to speak to grace-walking, mature Christians as you seek to carry out your Father's will for your life.

Don't misunderstand—I think there are rare occasions when God speaks so clearly and so certainly about major life-changing decisions that we don't need to ask anything from anybody. But that is the exception. The default setting of a Christian who is comfortable with his identity will often include asking counsel from other godly people.

Now, I'm not talking about taking a poll among all your friends. Some people err in that direction. They'll go ask all their friends and take a vote to try to determine God's will. That's not appropriate either.

What I am talking about is sharing with other trusted confidants what *you* believe God is saying to you, and finding out if they sense God working in the same way. Yes, you have the mind of Christ, but the treasure is in "an earthen vessel." We aren't infallible, so it is always a good idea to see if others we trust sense God's ways in what we are thinking.

### Laying Things Out with God and Others

I have several friends who know me intimately, with whom I share my struggles and my personal life. I share with them the major decisions I have to make, and I often ask their input because I value it. They know me. They know my desire to glorify God in my actions and my desire to fulfill His will.

I'll lay a scenario out and say, "Here's what I think the Lord is showing me. Here's what I'm thinking about it. I'm trusting the Lord, and I can't find that the things I'm thinking are contrary to His Word. What's your opinion?" I regularly get valuable feedback from these few close friends. I take their input very seriously. And I take it *doubly* seriously when I find they are all telling me the same thing.

We all need input from other Christians we respect. I also think that if you are married, *at the minimum* there ought to be a consensus between you and your spouse. The Bible is clear that a husband and wife are one, so if we are experiencing the mind of Christ we will be in agreement.

At least with major decisions, there should be agreement before you act on them. Since a husband and wife are one, I believe they should always act as one in the decisions of life. Since I was married in 1973, I have found that my wife, Melanie, has been my most trustworthy counselor.

One personal example is when I left the pastorate after almost 21 years. I had been a pastor from the time I was 19 years old and had planned to serve as a pastor of a local church all of my life. I couldn't imagine doing anything else. Then the time came when I began to gradually become aware that God might have a different path for me.

> I said to her, "This is what I think the Lord is saying and doing. What are your thoughts? What is God saying to you?"

I began to sense a compelling desire to resign so I could begin to teach the message of God's grace in many different places. Deep inside me, I felt it was what He wanted me to do. The first challenge in my mind revolved around how to share with my wife that I felt God was telling me to leave a stable place with a predictable income…and step out into "nothingness" with the hope that He would open doors for me to do what I thought He was putting into my heart.

Although I believed this was His will, I couldn't shake the feelings of fear that would regularly come over me. (Remember, where there is no room for doubt, there is no need for faith.) Melanie and I had four children at home. We had just built a new house, which had an accompanying new mortgage. Like most young families, we had car payments, medical expenses, school expenses, sons with insatiable appetites for food, and daughters whose needs were no less. Get the picture?

So it was no small decision for me to leave the work at a local church to take on the itinerant work I have now. I was not about to launch into this without Melanie's complete agreement. I knew she would share the same concerns I had.

So we spent much time discussing it. We prayed separately about it. We prayed together about it. I said to her, "This is what I think the Lord is saying and doing. What are your thoughts? What is God saying to you?" She prayed about it. After several months of discussion, exploration, and prayer, we jointly moved forward into the new phase of life we're still in today. We only resigned the pastorate and set out on this path after God had clearly spoken to both of us.

## My Advice to Married Couples

"So what if God had spoken to you and not to her?" some people have asked me. "Then I wouldn't have done it," I reply. "Not until God had spoken to her. He is capable of talking to her. Her heart is open to Him." So I would say to a married couple, "Don't make major life changes until you both are in agreement—because God is able to speak to you both."

Men, don't take some kind of dictatorial approach, like one man I met. Roger told me, "*I'm* the head of my house. *I'm* the one who leads, and my wife follows. That's what the Bible says."

"Do you know something else the Bible says?" I asked him. "In Ephesians 5, it says, 'Be subject *to one another* in the fear of Christ.' What are your thoughts on that verse?"

"I'm not going to argue with you," Roger answered. "The biblical way has always been for wives to be submissive. That's what we will honor in my house."

I won't allow myself to get sidetracked by a discussion of submission in marriage here, but the point that the Bible teaches the value of mutual submission in marriage deserves consideration. When we are confident in who we are and in who God is, we don't have to impose an authoritarian decision on our wives. Love your wife by respecting her, and wait for the Holy Spirit to speak to her before you act. While it is admirable for a wife to trust her husband's judgment, it is equally admirable for him to trust hers.

I've come to realize that when my wife is hesitant about some decision I think is right, I need to wait. I should wait until either the Lord speaks to her on the issue, or I come to the conclusion I was wrong in what I was thinking. I've been prevented from making some serious mistakes by listening to my wife. I would encourage you to do the same in your marriage. He can speak to you from your wife's mouth as easily as He can speak in your thoughts.

## Factor #4: God's Will Can Usually Be Detected Through Surrounding Circumstances

In considering our circumstances, it's important to learn to see the value of God's timing. Keep your eyes open. Wait for right circumstances to validate the decision. The right thing done at the wrong time can create disaster. The Bible says, "The steps of a man are established by the Lord" (Psalm 37:23). A mature Christian looks at circumstances to see if God is outwardly validating what He appears to be doing inwardly.

Remember, I'm not giving you a list of steps on how to know the will of God. Jesus living through you *is* the will of God. I am trying to give you a practical framework for understanding what Christ in you is doing. The thoughts you have often arise as a result of the things you see around you. He will put His thoughts in you by showing you evidence of His work in the surrounding details.

Looking at your circumstances and seeing what Christ is doing there is important. Many a Christian has been sidetracked by ignoring God-designed circumstances and pushing forward in an impulsive immaturity that he, rightly or wrongly, might be calling "faith."

I married when I was 19 years old. Melanie was 18. After about a year, I got the idea the Lord wanted us to leave our home and move to a faraway state to join another ministry. I made the mistake of not waiting for the Lord to confirm it and make it clear. Back then I didn't know these things I'm sharing with you, nor about how to allow Christ to express His life through me.

It's embarrassing to tell, but here's what I did. I sold everything we owned. Everything! I was so ready to make this move, so confident that this was the will of God. Then, after selling everything we owned, I received a letter from the ministry saying, "Thanks, but no thanks. We don't need you."

Ohhh…if only I had known then the advice from God's Word I'm sharing with you now! I ignored my circumstances, and I paid a price for it. I didn't wait until my wife was in full agreement, and I paid a price for it. I wasn't thinking the thoughts of Christ. I wasn't applying the wisdom I now know, and I paid the price for it. Learn from me. We need to make sure the Lord is working in our circumstances.

## Factor #5: Abandon Any Personal Agenda

Understanding God's will for your life means you know that Christ *is* your life, and you are willing to accept anything He might purpose for you. It means laying aside selfish plans and being willing to accept anything He wants. To think His thoughts means that I turn my back on my own independence.

I remember once, years ago, when I served as pastor of a small local church, circumstances became very difficult for me there. I began to pray, "Lord, I want Your will to be done"—which really meant, "Lord, I want to leave this place and go to a more peaceful and, preferably, larger one." God in His goodness wouldn't honor that. He left me there until I abandoned my plan and was willing to receive His plan. Little by little, I moved away from my own agenda and submitted myself to *His* plan for me.

To be confident that He is guiding your thoughts, it is important to give up the notion that you have to make something happen. That's back to the control issue. Let it go and trust Him.

❈

I want to challenge you as you think through the decisions you face in your own life today. Don't approach the decision-making process from a legalistic standpoint. Determine to know God's will from a grace standpoint, knowing that He wants to guide you, and He will. Every one of the five factors we have considered in this chapter focuses on the Person of Jesus Christ, who *is* the will of God for you. Trust *Him*—and He will put the thoughts in your mind that will lead you to the place He has planned for you.

## ❈ G. R. A. C. E. GROUP QUESTIONS ❈

1. Read John 15:1-5. What is the difference between *producing* fruit and *bearing* fruit? What is the main point Jesus was making in this explanation of the vine and the branches? How does that principle apply to your fulfilling God's will for you?

2. Explain, in your own words, what it means to rest in Christ. How can people tell when they are resting in Him and when they have taken matters into their own hands? Why is it true that our flesh always struggles to be in control of our environment? Read Galatians 5:16-18, and discuss how trying to be in control of our own lives is to be trapped in legalism and to fight against God's will for our lives.

3. What would you say to a friend who tells you that God is leading him to do something that is clearly opposed to what the Bible says? What would your answer be if the person said, "Yes, but I'm under grace!"

4. Who are the people in your life that you trust to tell you the truth when you are facing major decisions and would benefit from honest input? If you are married, when is a time you and your mate disagreed about God's will for you in a particular matter? How was the issue resolved? What is the biblical way to move through such times?

5. When is a time you ignored circumstantial evidence of what God was showing you about His plan for you? What was the result? Read the story in Acts 27 of the shipwreck of Paul and his companions. What factors led to their fate? What lessons can be learned from this chapter about knowing God's will for our own lives?

6. Identify an incident in Scripture when a follower of God allowed his own personal agenda to take priority over what God planned for him or her. What was the outcome? How did the Lord respond to their choice?

# CHAPTER 5

# Lighten Up

YOU'VE PROBABLY HEARD OF THE "KISS Principle," which suggests, "Keep It Simple, Stupid!" The point made is that simplicity should be the primary approach to matters, and complexity should be avoided as much as possible. For our purpose here, I'd like to baptize that harsh saying and change it to "Keep It Spiritually Simple."

In his well-known book *Experiencing God,* Henry Blackaby shares an illustration that shows us how to keep things simple. It encouraged me about knowing God's will when I was struggling with whether or not to leave the pastorate. Blackaby suggests that if you plan to drive somewhere and don't know where you are going, there are two ways by which you might reach your destination. (And let's assume you have no means of remote communication.)

First, you might approach somebody and ask him to give you a map. Maybe he'll highlight it for you. Maybe he'll say, "Go up this interstate, turn off this exit, go so many miles until you come to this country road." (Please, just don't speak compass!) The gist of his message is, "Follow these directions, and you'll reach your destination."

The second way you could reach your destination is to approach someone and ask him, instead of giving you instructions, to get in the car with you and take you where you want to go. In this way he will *be* your map. He will give you directions as you drive. In the first instance, you would *have* a map given by someone. In the second, your new friend would *become* the map.

Religious legalism says, "The Bible is a map you come to so you can learn what to *do*"—but you are left on your own to follow it. When I lived under law as a Christian legalist, I was very sincere about making the right choices. I would come to the Bible and read it, but there was a problem. I couldn't find the exact answers for all the choices I had to make. I wanted to do God's will, but it wasn't an easy or straightforward thing to know how to do.

Religion complicates nearly all aspects of a life that Christ specifically said was to be *easy*. In Matthew 11:29-30, Jesus invites us to take His yoke as our own, but contrary to the mental picture that may come to mind, He says, "My yoke is easy and My burden is light." *The Message* puts it this way: "Walk with me and work with me—watch how I do it. Learn the unforced rhythms of grace. I won't lay anything heavy or ill-fitting on you."

The plan God has for you isn't hard to know or to do once you "learn the unforced rhythms of grace." God's purpose for His children is really very simple. His desire for us is that we relax and let Him guide us through life one step at a time.

> For many years, I put all my focus on "doing the right thing." That's what most Christians focus on constantly.

Have you thought of the will of God as something hard to find and even harder to do? I hope you're beginning to see by this point in our study that it isn't that way at all. Ironically, it is our struggle to accomplish something easy that creates the stress so many Christians experience about God's will for their lives.

Remember that Jesus said that just as we abide in Him, He abides in us. Are you beginning to imagine the possibilities you possess because of Jesus Christ literally living His life through you? If Christ animated your thoughts and actions, how often would you get out of the will of God then? How often would you be *in* the will of God?

Living through you is exactly what Jesus is willing to do if you will just relax, depend on Him, and trust Him to animate the actions of your life. We might say, then, that Jesus Christ *is* the will of God for your life. This becomes a recognized reality in us as we calmly rest in Him, living out of our true identity. We can trust that He will express God's plan *for* us, *through* us, day by day.

For many years, I put all my focus on "doing the right thing." That's what most Christians focus on constantly. They think that the will of God is doing the exact right thing.

Legalism suggests that the Christian walk is all about finding that right thing and doing it. But all this emphasis on finding and doing the exact right thing builds tremendous pressure and creates enormous fear. How can we be sure that we have found what that exact right thing is? What horrible consequences might we suffer by missing it?

Experiencing the grace walk is different. Grace teaches us that we are to focus on Jesus Christ and what He has done, not on ourselves and what we need to do. (It's important to remember that we are not "human *do*ings" but "human *be*ings.") By now, I hope you have learned that when we know Christ is our Life, our doing flows out of our being in Him and He in us.

Some people have made knowing and doing God's will so hard that the best thing they can do for both themselves and for the glory of God is to *lighten up*. Life isn't a test—it's a rest. We simply rest in Christ, and He handles life through us.

The script of the story of your life has been written from start to finish. Don't worry. You've been given the part and it won't be taken away. And you don't even have to figure out the storyline. The Director will patiently and even lovingly guide you one scene at a time until the final curtain. So relax and enjoy the show. Not only is it not your job to write the story (remember, it has already been written), you don't even have to know how it ends. The Producer has already finished and it is "in the can"—so just go with the flow.

## Personal Guidance into God's Will

Wanda came home from college one weekend, and I ran into her at church. "You know, I've been praying to know God's will about finding the man He wants me to marry," she told me in a lighthearted way.

"Yes, I know. How's it going?" I asked.

"Well, I have *finally* found the exact verse that speaks to me about this whole thing."

"Oh, really? What is it?"

With a twinkle in her eye she answered, "If any man will come after me, let him!"

Of course, Wanda was joking. But the fact is, Christians do run into a struggle all the time when they try to use the Bible like a road map for life. To Wanda's dismay, there is no Bible verse that will tell a person who to marry. Neither are there any verses that will tell you where to go to college, what occupation to pursue, or where to live. And yet, we all still need to make decisions like those, and a thousand smaller ones, every day.

It is always frustrating to use the Bible to look for answers this way, because the Bible doesn't address specific things like these. Consequently, people often resort to purely subjective interpretations, reading what they want *into* the Bible. They'll get out of it whatever they have been programmed to get out of their reading. While the Bible is certainly objective, our application of it to our lives often isn't.

When you sincerely want to know Christ and live in a way that is pleasing to Him, you won't be satisfied with that approach. Please don't misunderstand me. The Bible *does* give us instruction and guidance. We have already seen that the Word of God is very important in understanding the will of God. It is filled with wisdom and practical instruction for living…but God is not limited to the Bible alone. It is so much better than that. The Bible is not our map or our instruction manual. *Jesus* is our map. Jesus Christ "gets into the car with us." *He* becomes our guide.

Therefore, to do the will of God, it is helpful to understand that it is primarily a Person, not a path. The will of God is Jesus. Again, as we have seen in earlier chapters, it's all about Him.

If you aren't trusting Christ to live through you, then all of your actions are going to be animated by your flesh—you acting out of your own independent strength and abilities. When that is the case, one decision is as good as another—or, to be more exact, as bad as another. If you aren't going to trust Christ to be who He is in you and through you, and if you aren't going to appropriate your identity in Him, it really makes little difference which choice you make. It is not about choosing the right path. It is about choosing the right Person, Jesus.

Do you want to do God's will? Then stop struggling. Lighten up, and let Jesus live through you. Based on an understanding of your identity in Christ, move forward through your decisions with confidence that He will guide your steps—and He will!

## Keeping It Simple

Knowing God's will is simple, really. We just choose to focus on Jesus Christ, who lives in us, trust that He is guiding our thoughts and giving us our desires, and move forward. Contrary to what you may have been taught or believed, this isn't complicated.

Rod came to me one day to discuss this issue. He had recently accepted a management position within his company. The promotion had seemed to be a good thing at first. He was paid what he initially thought would be a good salary, but in recent months he had come to wonder whether or not he had made the right decision.

"When I accepted this salaried position, I thought it would be a good change from the slot I was in before, where I got paid by the hour," he began. "What I didn't realize is that I would have to put in so many hours. When I was paid on an hourly basis, I actually made more money by working overtime than I do now. And I had the choice then as to when I would accept overtime hours and when I would say no. Now I don't have a choice. The job has to be done, and I get paid the same whether I work forty hours or sixty hours a week. I'm wondering if I made the right decision now. I thought God was opening a door for me, but now I'm not so sure. I've prayed and prayed about it. I've tried to get guidance from the Bible, but I haven't figured out a thing about what I should do."

"What are your options now?" I asked.

"Well, my immediate supervisor actually told me I could go back to my old job if I want to. But I don't want management in the company to think I have no ambition."

"So you're concerned they would think less of you?"

"Yes—and in the long run, if another round of layoffs comes like has happened in the past, I may be one of the first they let go," he explained.

"How uncomfortable are you with the job you have now?"

"I hate it," Rod answered. "I can't imagine working under this kind of stress for years to come."

"Are you sure about that?" I continued.

"Positive," he replied. "There's no way I want to do this from now on."

"So, on the one hand you have the option of keeping on with a job you can't tolerate. On the other, you can go back to the job you enjoyed, with the understanding there *might* be negative repercussions from your choice. Then again, maybe there won't be. Am I right?"

"Yes, that's right."

"So it's a definite thing that you'd hate staying in this position, but only a possibility something bad could happen if you change back to your old job."

"Yes," Rod confirmed.

"Are you open to my viewpoint?" I asked.

"Of course. That's why I came to talk to you."

"Rod, I think you should consider backtracking and going back to the old position. You've indicated you *know* you'll hate staying in this one. Your supervisor has told you you can move back to your old spot. The only reason for believing that anything negative could come from that move is an abstract fear in your mind about what *might* happen, but that also might never happen. And even if it did, God would guide your next steps at that moment."

"I think you're right," Rod answered slowly. "I've been overthinking this thing...way too much."

The problem that Rod faced was one that holds many people in slavery to bad situations. Remember, KISS— Keep It Spiritually Simple. We just choose to focus on Jesus Christ, who lives in us, and trust that He is guiding our thoughts, that He is giving us our desires—and move forward.

> Don't complicate life by believing you are trying to find your way through a maze of options.

Rod was so focused on doing the right thing that he had temporarily lost his focus on Christ. He had forgotten the fact that Christ really will guide our thoughts. He will be the one who puts our desires in us as we depend on Him.

Don't complicate your life by overthinking your circumstances. The essence of all of life is your relationship with Christ. It's not about walking a tightrope where you absolutely must make perfect decisions at every step. Your life is a relationship to be enjoyed. You weren't born to *do something*. You were born to *know Somebody*. Everything else will flow out of that.

In the great prayer He offered on our behalf, Jesus Himself gave the definition: "This is eternal life, that they may know You, the only true God, and Jesus Christ whom You have sent" (John 17:3). *Knowing Him*—that's it. God's will for your life will naturally come from recognizing that His life is inside you and that He will guide your thoughts and desires. He will move you forward, even when it sometimes looks like you're going backward, as Rod experienced.

Keep it simple! Don't complicate life by believing you are trying to find your way through a maze of options. Jesus defined the meaning of life in terms of a relationship. It is about *knowing God and His Son Jesus Christ*. Later in Scripture, the apostle Paul explained that, despite all his religious credentials and enviable achievements, they were nothing compared to knowing Christ:

> Whatever things were gain to me, those things I have counted as loss for the sake of Christ. More than that, I count all things to be loss in view of the surpassing value of knowing Christ Jesus my Lord, for whom I have suffered the loss of all things, and count them but rubbish so that I may gain Christ…that I may know Him (Philippians 3:7-8,10).

## Everything Centers on Christ

There have been many religious founders, teachers, gurus, and philosophers in the history of the world. All of them have taught moral laws, words of wisdom, and doctrines, saying, in effect, "Go this way." Jesus Christ, in contrast, is unique. The center of His teaching was not "Keep these rules," "Go this way," or "Follow these practices." Jesus always pointed to *Himself* and simply said, *"Follow me."*

You have been created in Christ as a unique expression of His life. The beauty of our God is so immense and awe-inspiring that He has shared Himself with us all in order to reveal Himself in this world through His body, the church. And each of us has an opportunity to show His life in a way that is unique to us. You have the ability to demonstrate the Christ-Life in a way that is different from anybody who has ever lived or ever will live because there will never be another you!

The idea of manifesting divine life through your lifestyle doesn't have to be an intimidating thought—when you realize that the only thing necessary is to trust God, relax, and just move forward into your destiny. His will for your life isn't something that contradicts who you are. Rather than going against the grain, it fits you perfectly. Lighten up! Relax and be yourself, because who you are is just right! After all, an omnipotent God created you!

The new you has been created in Christ Jesus so that His life fits you like a hand in a glove. He made you to be who you are so He can show

Himself to the world through your temperament, your personality...all the aspects of who you are that make you uniquely you! "Christ in you, the hope of glory," wrote the apostle Paul. What an awesome thought it is to know that Jesus Christ lives in you and through you!

## Simple Questions You Can Ask Yourself

Andrea came in to talk to me one day. "I want to do God's will," she said, "but I don't have any idea what He wants me to do with my life. What about people like me who don't have great dreams? Sometimes I feel like something must be wrong with me because I don't feel a strong sense I need to move in *any* particular direction."

Andrea's concern isn't that uncommon. There are many sincere Christians who want to do God's will but don't know where to even begin. They would say they don't sense His leading them in one direction more than another. They often feel like something is wrong with them because they can't identify a big dream they have for their lives, one they believe is from God.

Maybe you find yourself in that category. How can you begin to determine God's will without having a clue of what that might be? There are two simple indicators that are often useful in beginning to understand the specific plan He has.

**1. Interests.** What interests you in life? It's often been asked, "If money were not a factor in your decision, what would you want to spend your life doing?" It's a good question. Your heavenly Father's plan for your life will very likely line up with what interests you.

Did you know it isn't coincidental that you find interest in the things that attract you? God Himself has programmed our interests as Christians into us. The Bible says, "Delight yourself in the LORD; and He will give you the desires of your heart" (Psalm 37:4). This verse teaches that God is the one who places the desires that are in your heart there. I don't think the verse is simply saying He will give you what you want, but rather that your wants are determined by Him. He deposits your desires within you. When God is the one who places your desires in you, He then delights to give you what you desire!

Have you considered the idea that God has placed your desires in you? Some people have such a distorted concept of God that they can't imagine His plan for them might actually be something that interests them and that they would enjoy. Maybe it's time to lighten up and realize that when you know your true identity, you can trust—trust that your thoughts and desires are the thoughts and desires of the Christ who lives inside you.

**2. Strengths.** What are the strengths you possess? Every Christian has been uniquely given gifts of particular strengths. If you don't recognize your gifts, it may be because you have never felt the confidence to explore them.

It may be important for you to identify your interests and then move forward to test your ability in those areas. Don't worry about failing. Because you know who you are in Christ, success or failure in a particular endeavor says nothing about your value. You are simply stretching your wings so you can learn to fly.

Don't allow insecurities about not being great at something keep you from trying. I once read that the woods would be very silent if no birds sang except those who sing best. God will enable you to develop your abilities as you go along. Right now, the task is to discover them.

If you are simply at a dead end on identifying your abilities, ask those who love you what they see as your strengths. See if what they say resonates with you. Sometimes, others can see us more objectively than we can see ourselves. Of course, at each step along the way, you will have been asking the Holy Spirit to guide you and show you your strengths.

As I shared these indicators with Andrea, I asked her two questions: 1) What do you enjoy doing? 2) What would your friends say is your strong suit?

Without hesitation, she answered, "I love to cook. I'm in my element when I have a crowd coming over for dinner and I'm able to prepare a nice meal. I go all out with it because I really enjoy it."

"Have you ever thought about moving in that direction with a greater amount of your time and energy?" I asked her.

"I'd love to," she answered. "I think I could make money at it, but I couldn't make as much as I do on my job now—and we need the income."

"Well, maybe if you pray about it and keep your antenna up, the Lord will show you how to do it," I answered. "He'll make it clear if this is it and show you how to move in that direction, if it's His will," I said.

Several months later, I ran into Andrea at the mall. "Guess what I'm doing to earn money now?" she excitedly asked me.

"Don't tell me you're catering meals already!" I answered.

"No, not that," she replied, "but I am baking wedding cakes and catering wedding receptions. It's something I'm doing on the weekends, but the word is getting out, and I'm hoping it will eventually turn into a full-time job!"

I was so happy to hear how Andrea was moving slowly, but surely, toward the fulfillment of a dream that would be so rewarding to her. It had all started by her yielding herself to Christ and trusting that the desires and thoughts she was having were indeed from God. Then she began to act on those internal promptings.

## Proving Out God's Will

Andrea's situation calls our attention back to Romans 12:1-2. This passage is powerful because it assures us we don't have to go through life guessing whether or not we are fulfilling God's will. It's not meant to be hard. Instead, there is an easy way:

> I urge you, brethren, by the mercies of God, to present your bodies a living and holy sacrifice, acceptable to God, which is your spiritual service of worship. And do not be conformed to this world, but be transformed by the renewing of your mind, so that you may prove what the will of God is, that which is good and acceptable and perfect.

These verses give us three aspects of knowing the will of God with certainty. It happens without any struggle on our part, as we simply respond to Him. First, we present ourselves completely to Him. Secondly, we are not being conformed to this world. And last, we are being transformed by the renewing of our minds. The passage says that we will then be able to "prove" what the will of God is.

Many Christians get bogged down in the place of indecision because they're afraid they might miss the will of God in the matters of their daily lives. This is an unfounded fear, because the Bible tells us we can *prove* the will of God—that is, we can put our decision-making to the test in a given matter and be assured that God will make His will apparent.

## Presenting Yourself to God

Paul begins by describing how we present ourselves to God. When you yield yourself to Him, your Father readily responds to you because you are the exact kind of sacrifice He loves—a living and holy sacrifice. To live out this verse, it is important to be clear about what it *isn't* saying, because many have misunderstood it. This verse is not saying that you have to make yourself holy in order to present yourself to God.

I used to teach that, if we want to know God's will, we had better make sure we become holy before we come to Him to find out His plan for us. I reasoned that, if God was going to work with me in fulfilling any kind of spiritual plan, I needed to first get my spiritual act together. I suspect there are many people who share that misguided viewpoint. Of course, in my legalistic lunacy, I could have named a dozen things I believed Christians must do to make that happen. Things like daily Bible reading and prayer, as well as many other things I thought made us more holy.

The fallacy in what I taught then was that I missed an obvious fact. We don't make ourselves holy. We can't. It isn't possible for a number of reasons, not the least of which is this: God has *already* made us holy in Christ! First Corinthians 3:16 says, "The temple of God is holy, and that is what you *are*."

Ty is a successful financial planner. Almost all of his clients are very wealthy people—"high rollers," he calls them. For a long time, Ty felt guilty over the idea of boldly pursuing clients at that financial level. "I was selling term life insurance and squeaking out a living," he said. "I dreamed of moving upward into a more lucrative role in finances, but believed that before God could bless me professionally, I needed to do some housekeeping spiritually."

Ty attended a conference I taught on what it means to experience the grace walk in life, and his thinking was transformed. "I learned I am already as holy as I'll ever be because Christ is my life," he said. "That one revelation was enough to empower me to know that God really is on my side. Because of that fact, I found myself moving forward more boldly than I had ever done before. I was motivated to pursue the additional training necessary to get certification and launch my own financial-planning practice."

> Believers are already holy because of our union with Christ, not because of anything we do or don't do.

The thing that empowered Ty to experience God's plan for his life was the understanding that he didn't have to improve himself spiritually. Through Christ, he was already the kind of person God delights to bless. Believers are already holy because of our union with Christ, not because of anything we do or don't do. The instruction here simply calls on us to abandon ourselves—"our-holy-selves," so to speak—totally into God's sovereign and omnipotent hands, trusting Him to guide us.

Note that the same verse that says we present ourselves as a holy sacrifice also says that we present ourselves as a *living* sacrifice. Though I taught that we must become holy before we could prove God's will, I never suggested that we needed to become *alive*. Why? Because I knew I was alive. I just didn't know I was holy. The Bible teaches, though, that we are both. Neither is because of what we do, but because of what He has already done.

## Relying on Your God-Given Holiness

Do you see this truth about yourself? You are *holy*! It isn't that you ought to be, or that you could be, or that one day you will be. You are, right now, the righteousness of God in Christ. That all took place because of the finished work of Christ at the cross.

You no more make yourself holy than you've made yourself alive. Both came from Him. So you can lighten up about who you are, knowing that who you are is exactly who God has made you to be. That being the case, you can be assured He wants to make His will known to you without your having to try to improve yourself. Don't complicate matters by thinking you need to do something.

Not knowing who we are in Christ can keep Christians from totally yielding themselves and their circumstances to God. After all, if we feel dirty, we certainly can't imagine that God is eager to show us His will for our lives. We question how He could use us at all, and whether He even wants to be around us.

On the other hand, because you know you are holy, you can come boldly before your Father and yield yourself to Him with the confidence that His will will manifest itself naturally as you test it by putting it into action. Remember, the apostle Paul isn't saying in this text that you have to become holy in order to prove out God's will for your life. To the contrary, he is saying that it is precisely because you *are* holy that you can know with certainty that He will make His will apparent.

Because we understand who God is and who we are, and because we understand our relationship with Him, we gladly surrender our lives to Him, trusting His love, goodness, and mercy to us in Jesus Christ! We know that His will is going to become apparent because, in Christ, we meet all the necessary conditions for knowing and doing the Father's will.

## Living as a Nonconformist

As we present ourselves to God, the Scripture says, "Do not be conformed to this world." What does it mean by "conformed"? It causes me to think of times I've seen concrete workers prepare to pour a driveway or sidewalk. The first thing they do is to build a form that will hold the concrete so it will take the shape they have designed.

That's what the world tries to do to us—even the religious world does it. Structures are laid out, and we are taught to stay within the bounds set for us. "If you want to know God's will, there are certain things *you must do.* You have to do your part." So we are told.

If you act outside those bounds, you will be sanctioned. Jesus ran into this challenge constantly. Everybody, including the religious world of His day, thought He had lost His mind, because He didn't go with the flow of how they believed things ought to be. He was a nonconformist, and his nonconformity provoked those around Him.

Paul is telling us something very important about how to know God's will with certainty. It's this: Don't stay inside the world's form. Don't be *con* (with) *formed* by the world. Get outside the box they have built for you. You don't have to jump through a series of religious hoops to know God's will. That's nothing but a bunch of religious hype. The Bible says that apart from God doing His work in us, our attitudes and actions will be formed by others. How we think and how we live will take shape around influences other than Christ.

What practical implication does this biblical nonconformity have on your potential to know God's will for your own life? The answer to that question varies from person to person. What prerequisites have you been told are necessary for you to know God's will? I've already given you one that I taught for years—that you should become holy... although, in reality, you already are.

What other ideas have "formed" the way you have thought about how to know God's will—ideas that you now realize are wrong? Remember, knowing God's will isn't a hard thing. Religion will try to make it that way, but your loving Father certainly has no part of that. His yoke is easy.

In another passage, Paul warns against being taken captive.

See to it that no one takes you captive through philosophy

and empty deception, according to the tradition of men, according to the elementary principles of the world, rather than according to Christ (Colossians 2:8).

We take on the philosophies, beliefs, values, and habits of the worldly and religious cultures in which we live. There are many traditions we are taught are necessary to know God's will, but many of them are empty deceptions consisting of the philosophy of man. If we allow it, these will influence the way we think about God's will. They aren't His way, but they attract those who believe knowing His will is a hard thing.

It is interesting to see how many Christians take a defensive stance against the *behaviors* of the culture around us—dress, music, entertainment, or other external things—while seeming to remain unaware of the dangers of the *ideas* of the world. And yet, from our thinking flow all the rest of our life's decisions and actions. We must be aware and on guard, because the worlds of both the unrighteous and the self-righteous will surely try to conform us to their shape.

## Moving Ahead as Transformed People

Do you remember Trans World Airlines? Their name reflected their flight routes. They flew *across* (trans) the world. That's how the Bible says we are to live here. A mold has been poured in which we are told to stay but, by the power of Christ, we have been set free and enabled to step *across* the form laid out for us. We are transformed people, who don't approach life the way others do.

As you live as a transformed person, you will see God's will for you emerge naturally. God Himself will see to it. Don't buy into the snake oil they are trying to sell you. Being confident of His will is easy when

> Your role is to yield yourself to Him. Don't allow others to complicate this for you.

you trust the Christ within you who is the very personification of God's will for your life.

Don't get bogged down. This isn't rocket science. You don't have to be a theologian or a genius to know what God wants you to do. Consider the questions raised in this chapter as a starting place. What do you *want* to do? What are your interests? What are your strengths?

If you move ahead with both your heart and your eyes wide open, the Holy Spirit will make it clear to you where to go and what to do next. Just live one day at a time, trusting Him to make it all clear in His way and His timing. The big picture will most definitely start to become clear to you.

Your role is to yield yourself to Him. Don't allow others to complicate this for you. Step across the traditional, demanding methods you've been told reveal God's will—and just live in simple faith in Christ. When the "fullness of time" according to God's agenda comes, you will discover the plan He has for you growing in your heart and being made evident in your circumstances.

### ❄ G. R. A. C. E. GROUP QUESTIONS ❄

1. Discuss the following statement: "The Bible is not primarily intended to be a *guide* book, but is meant to be a *grace* book." While it is true we can find guidance in the Bible, there are numerous dangers in seeing it as nothing more than an instruction manual for knowing how we are to live. What does John 5:39 teach us about this matter?

2. Recall the story in this chapter about Rod, who was afraid of a job change because it might lead to negative results. What is a time in your life when you allowed fear to keep you from making a choice you might have benefited from? How does Romans 8:15 apply to situations like this?

3. Andrea began to bake wedding cakes and cater weddings when she allowed herself to move toward her interests and strengths. If money were not an object, what would you want to spend your time doing? How might you begin to express your own strengths and interests to a greater degree?

4. Discuss Romans 12:1-2 and how we can *prove* God's will for our lives by applying the truths taught in those two verses.

5. Identify some of the renowned Christians of the past who stepped out of the mold set for them and, consequently, found God's will for their lives. Who are some Bible characters who did the same thing?

6. In what areas of your life would it be helpful for you to "lighten up"?

CHAPTER 6

# Follow Your Heart

"PLEASE PRAY FOR US that we will know the right decision to make," Larry asked the small group that met in his home. "We believe that taking the job I've been offered in Dallas is the right thing, but we want to make doubly sure we aren't missing God's will. You know how deceptive the devil can be. I don't want to be misled by him. The way he deceives us sometimes is so insidious, and I don't want to be fooled. We know he is cunning, and we really want to hear from God on this situation."

As Larry talked, it began to sound like the time had been set aside to honor Satan himself. More was said about the devil's ability to mislead us than anything else. Of course, there is no doubt that Larry's sincere desire was to know and do God's will, but listening to the way he talked, you'd think that the ability of the enemy to deceive us is greater than God's ability to keep us in His will.

Larry is no different than many Christians today. They live a life filled with fear that they're going to do the wrong thing. They tiptoe through this world like scared little kids in a haunted house. I meet them all the time. They say, "Steve, pray for me. Pray that I won't miss the will of God." Or, "Satan is so powerful and so deceptive. Pray for me. I don't want to miss the will of God." Or, "I want to stay in the center of God's perfect will. I can be deceived and make a mess of my life if I go out there apart from God's will." They go on and on about the ability of the enemy to deceive them. When they do make decisions, they're so scared they're going to miss God's will that they're always timid, tentative, and unsure.

When it comes to making decisions regarding God's will, many Christians seem to abandon faith altogether. Instead, they express great fear that they're going to miss His will. Their fear so handicaps them that they sometimes do practically nothing of any real spiritual significance. They'd rather do nothing than take the risk of making a mistake.

## The Trap of Analysis Paralysis

Believers who fall into this kind of thinking are victims of one of the enemy's greatest weapons—*analysis paralysis*. I don't know who coined that term, but it clearly describes how many people live their lives. But the solution to the problem isn't complicated. Grace never is, if we will just accept the simple truth.

Think of it this way: Imagine that you're standing in the center of a large field. You can see the horizon all around you in every direction. Ahead, you can see the ocean, with the waves lapping up on the shore. Off to one side, in another direction, you can see a mountain range with snow-covered peaks. Behind you is a meadow filled with wildflowers, and you see the breeze gently blowing across the field. To the other side of you is a forest, where you can see the sunlight filtering down through the trees. There's a different scene in every direction.

You know that somewhere off in the distance is the place God has for you, where His perfect will for you can be found. But how can you know that place, and how can you get there? With virtually infinite choices, how can you know the one place God has planned for you?

Some people would stand in that one spot in the field for the rest of their lives because they're afraid. They believe there's one spot God wants them to be, and if they miss that one spot, they will be out of the will of God for the rest of their lives. They hold this legalistic mind-set, believing it is entirely *up to them* to find out what God's will is.

"Why do you call that legalistic?" you might ask. In answer, let me remind you of the difference between law and grace. Under the system of legalism, we make spiritual progress or gain God's blessings based on what *we* do. That's law.

On the other hand, grace says that God will bless us because we are in Jesus Christ, who has already done everything—and for no other reason at all. That's grace.

Legalism insists that knowing and doing the will of God is all up to you. It says, "Yes, you'd better weigh out all your options, because you don't want to miss the will of God. You'd better make sure because, of all the places you could go, there's only one right place for you. And if you miss that, you may have to settle for God's second-best—or worse!

> Fear is the opposite of faith, and it paralyzes us. That's why it is one of Satan's greatest weapons against the Christian.

"You may go north when you should have gone east, and you'll be out of God's will. Or you might go north when you should have gone south, and boy!—*then* you will be in the exact opposite place from where God wants you! You'd better find the exact center of God's will. You'd better seek it out and find it, and you'd better do it right!" That's a mind filled with legalism doing the talking. And assuming we *can* find the one right choice, by what power can we then do it? Legalism always puts the entire burden on *us*.

Maybe you are one of these kind of people. You've experienced fear-driven analysis paralysis, and you've been out in the middle of the field for years, petrified. You've not moved in any direction, because you're afraid you're going to make a mistake.

Nothing great has ever been accomplished by those who are

dominated by fear. Fear is the opposite of faith, and it paralyzes us. That's why it is one of Satan's greatest weapons against the Christian. When motivated by fear, not only are we driven away from trusting in Christ, we lose our ability to reason and to think clearly. Either we tend to do foolish things, or we are paralyzed and do nothing. Either way, the devil has made us ineffective.

The prayer request Larry shared with his small group *sounded* spiritual, but his strong emphasis on the enemy's ability to deceive betrayed his underlying fears. To confidently move toward fulfilling God's plan for him in a way that would bring a sense of joy, even a sense of divine destiny, Larry needed to let go of his hidden worries about missing God's will, which seemed to consume him, and get on with the business of trusting his heart and *doing* God's will.

## The Fear of Messing Up

"So," you might ask, "how *do* I find God's will for my life?" As I've mentioned, I used to go about it in any number of ways. I would think, *If I only prayed enough…fasted enough…read my Bible enough.* Are you beginning to see how that legalistic list dominated so many areas of my life? It's sinister how Satan uses things with which God intends to bless us to actually enslave us. As sincere as I was, my view of these activities actually prevented me often from confidently walking in His will. It's not that doing those things is wrong, in and of itself, but I thought they were the price I had to pay to get directions for my life path from God.

Having spent much time with many Christians in the evangelical and charismatic church world, I assure you this problem is common among Christians. One of the greatest factors that keeps Christians from boldly charging toward the agenda God has for them is a gnawing sense of guilt—guilt that they're not behaving well enough to know and do God's will. They don't know they can trust their heart's desires. It's pathetic. I know because I spent many years of my life struggling under the same debilitating delusion.

You don't have to be afraid you're going to mess up God's plan for your life, because it's not up to you to ensure that the plan is executed. It never has been. That's *His* job. Yours is to trust. The rest is up to Him.

Not knowing that fact, though, I would double up on my efforts to meet the list of demands I thought would move me toward the will of God. Then I would often write down all the pros and cons of making this choice or that choice. I was serious about figuring this thing out, and I wanted to prove it to God and to myself.

Again, I'm not saying there's anything wrong with doing those things if they're done for the right reasons. I am saying that if those are the things you are depending upon, if you're looking to those kinds of actions as the steps you have to climb to find God's perfect will for your life, you'll never be able to move forward with confidence.

## Finding God's Alternative to Fear

What is God's answer to this worry and paralysis? There is a great promise from His Word you should know: "God has not given us a spirit of timidity, but of power and love and discipline" (2 Timothy 1:7). There are important issues and applications in this verse. For one, the word translated "timidity" does not refer to all kinds of fear, because all kinds of fear aren't bad. Some feelings of fear are normal to the human experience and are useful for our protection.

For instance, if you were at the zoo and saw a lion that had escaped from its cage, it would be normal to feel fear. It would motivate you to take cover or run away. Fear is an important emotion to protect us from real, objective danger. However, that kind of fear is not destructive, and it is not the type against which the Bible warns us.

"Timidity" is a word that can also be translated *cowardice*. It means cringing, paralyzing fear. This refers to the fear that comes from our imaginations, especially imaginary scenarios of the future. It's fear that has no basis in truth. This kind of fear grows out of unbelief and is destructive. Notice that Paul says this kind of fear does *not* come from God. This kind of fear looks into circumstances or into the future and imagines God not being there. We are told not to give in to it.

On the positive side, Paul says that God *does* give us a spirit of "power and love." If you think through the decisions facing you, wouldn't you feel much more confident if you could make them being absolutely convinced your Father's love superintends your actions and His power enables you to move forward with them? The reality is, you do have that spirit—His Spirit, which God has given you.

As Larry's small-group leader began to encourage him in this area of truth, he began to grasp it. One evening a few weeks later he shared, "The Lord has been showing me something about myself lately. I have given way too much credit to the devil. I'm beginning to see that the Lord really does give me the desires of my heart. He's the one who puts them there—and if He puts them there, it's up to Him to see that those desires are fulfilled. I don't have to worry about being deceived. Protecting me from that is the Holy Spirit's business. All I need to do is trust Him." A spontaneous chorus of "Amen!" and "That's right!" from around the room confirmed that Larry had taken an important step in discovering the grace and freedom of God's plan for him.

### Discipline as God Intends It

The last characteristic of the spirit God gives us is also a wonderful one. "Discipline" is how the New American Standard Bible translates it. Now, certain words tend to evoke certain responses, and at first glance this one almost has a legalistic tone to it. The modern *misuse* of this word might make you think of putting your nose to the grindstone and pushing yourself to do what you ought to do while hating every minute of it.

That's not what "discipline" means. The King James version translates it as "a sound mind." Other versions render it "self-control." The essence of its meaning is the ability to eagerly and energetically put our minds to a task and stick with it until we see it finished. It is the characteristic of being resolved to finish what we start. What a great quality for daily living! This is exactly what God gives us through the indwelling Christ. Once He has caused us to know His will for our lives, He empowers us to pursue the fulfillment of His plan until we have fulfilled His desire for our lives right down to the smallest details. Not only does the Christ who lives inside you show you your Father's will, but He goes on to motivate and enable you to press on until you successfully accomplish it.

## Choose to Live by God's Resources

Given that God offers us Himself through the indwelling Holy Spirit, and given the promises Christ has made to be our sufficiency for living, the thing you might need to do is simple: Move out. Move out in faith. Just do it.

We all know the temptation that will come sometimes. (And here is where we *do* need to be alert for the evil one.) Fear continues to whine, "But what if I make a mistake?" Legalism declares that it's all up to you to find the exact right thing God has for you, the exact right place. Unbelief suggests that God hides His will from you, works at making it hard for you to find, and then blames you for not finding it.

How can we respond to this lie? We can confront it boldly. What an insult to the Holy Spirit who lives in us, to give in to that nagging sense of unbelief! What an insult to the indwelling Christ who guides us, and who has promised never to leave us or forsake us! What an insult to the sovereign God, who oversees everything that happens to us in every circumstance of life!

Instead of living in fear—cowardice—we can say, "Lord Jesus, I trust You. You died for me. You have promised to complete the work You began in me."

God loves you and is working out His good plan in your life. Thank God, you can meet these decisions sensing His presence and knowing He will fulfill His promises. And you can experience His power as He makes His will known to you.

Once you come to see the way Satan works in order to keep us living in fear, it is easy to see why the Bible describes him as a liar and an accuser. Slandering the character of God has been his method from day one, in order to tempt us to doubt God and distrust Him.

Knowledge of this inner battle with our flesh again emphasizes the importance of keeping our eyes on Christ. Jesus is God's grace in action, God's love embodied. Jesus is God's attitude toward us made audible and visible. God has proven His love for us by sending His Son to die for our sins, then raising Him from the dead, and now identifying us with Him. We are *in Christ*, with new eternal identities as children of God.

Therefore, we can *choose* to trust Him and walk ahead in our lives with unshakable confidence that our Father is working out His purpose for our lives. We can deny fear's voice and choose to trust Christ to be God's will for us. We can move forward, following our hearts.

## You Can Follow Your Heart

"This all sounds a little scary to me," Rachel said to me after hearing me teach on this subject. "I think following our hearts can be a dangerous thing."

"Why?" I asked.

"Because the Bible teaches that the heart is deceitful above all things and desperately wicked," she answered.

"Yes, but where is that found in the Bible?"

"I'm not sure. I think in Jeremiah."

"Rachel, you're right," I continued. "It's in Jeremiah 17:9, but the important thing about that verse is in what part of the Bible it's found."

"What do you mean?" she asked.

"I mean it's in the *Old Testament* and is a verse that doesn't apply to you as a New Testament Christian."

"But it's in the Bible," she pointed out.

"Yes, it is," I replied, "but to properly understand the Bible it is important to know that, while all of it is *for* us, not everything said in

> "God took care of that problem when you trusted Him for salvation."

it is *about* us. You don't have a wicked heart now. You used to, but God took care of that problem when you trusted Him for salvation."

## What the Scriptures Say About Your Heart

Rachel struggled with my suggestion that her heart wasn't evil until we discussed what the Bible goes on to say about the matter. Are you under the same impression she was? Do you believe your heart is deceitful and wicked? If so, I have some good news that is going to set you free from that kind of thinking. Look at this passage in Ezekiel 36:26-27:

> I will give you a new heart and put a new spirit within you; and I will remove the heart of stone from your flesh and give you a heart of flesh. I will put My Spirit within you and cause you to walk in My statutes, and you will be careful to observe My ordinances.

Remember that in the Old Testament, the Holy Spirit "came upon" people, but He didn't live in them. But the promise of God to His people under the Old Covenant was that a day was coming when He would give them a new heart by placing His Spirit *inside* them.

Has that day come yet? Consider yourself and your relationship to God's Spirit. Where does He live today? He lives *in* you! Yes, that day has come! When Jesus Christ died and rose again, the New Covenant became effectual. (See Hebrews 10:12-18 for confirmation of this.) The Spirit of God doesn't come *upon* you like He did in the Old Testament times. Instead, He has taken up permanent residence *inside* you, where He will abide with you forever (see John 14:16).

God has done in you exactly what He promised through Ezekiel that He would one day do. He has put His Spirit within you and has taken away that old, deceitful, desperately wicked heart. He has given you a new heart that yearns to honor Him!

"But I always thought that was something that happened when we got to heaven," Rachel objected when I told her this.

"The Bible doesn't say that," I answered. "It isn't after you get to heaven that God forgives your sins. It isn't after you get to heaven that He gives you His Spirit. It isn't after you get to heaven that He makes a 'new creation' out of you. All that happens at salvation. The same is true about receiving a new heart. Our dirty, deceitful heart is replaced by the life of Christ within us at the very moment we trust Him."

"I've just never thought of it that way," Rachel responded. "I've always thought that, deep down inside, I was still dirty. I've known God has forgiven me, but I still haven't felt clean."

## Dirt Doesn't Define Us

Rachel's problem is a common one. After all, we all know that we still sometimes have dirty thoughts and impure feelings, and still sometimes do sinful actions. The important thing to understand, however, is that *those things don't define us*. We are clean because of what Christ has done.

Why is this so important? If you think you're still rotten at the core, how are you going to ever be able to believe that God is going to show you the plan He has in mind for you? Don't believe that. You aren't dirty anymore. Just because you still get dirt *on* you doesn't mean it is *in* you.

A good illustration of this fact is an incident that happened with Jesus and His disciples when they were in the upper room together. He was about to wash the feet of the disciples. Peter protested over Jesus' assuming such a lowly position of servanthood and said to Him, "There is no way I'm going to let you wash my feet!" Jesus answered Him, "If you don't, you won't be involved in the plan I have in mind." Peter then blurted out, "Then go for it! Wash me from head to toe! I'm in!"

Jesus' response to Peter here is instructive. He said to him,

If you've had a bath in the morning, you only need your feet washed now and you're clean from head to toe. My concern, you understand, is holiness, not hygiene. So now you're clean (John 13:10 MSG).

The point Jesus was making was that Peter wasn't a dirty person. He simply had dirt on him at that moment, dirt that needed to be wiped off. There is a big difference between the two. Do you see it? Just because you sometimes get dirt (sinful thoughts, feelings, or even actions) on you doesn't mean that you've morphed into a dirty person.

One time many years ago, our family came out of the house to go to Sunday-morning church. As I turned to close the door, our small dog bolted out and ran across the yard. We were late, and I didn't have the time for that kind of nonsense.

Impatient, I took off across the yard yelling at our dog, which was on a mission to escape me. As I chased him down a slight slope, my foot hit a slick spot on the grass, which was still covered with morning dew. Down I went. Not just to the ground, but also down the hill...all the way down the hill the rolling reverend went. By the time I reached the bottom, I had mud and grass stains all over my clothes.

When I stood up, I came to an instant realization of four things I was absolutely certain of: 1) I wanted that dog to die. Now. 2) My family, laughing hysterically, didn't understand one iota about Christian compassion. 3) I could say the word I heard coming out of my mouth with no fear that my mother was around to punish me for saying it. 4) I looked filthy dirty.

The immediate challenge at that moment was number 4. I had dirt all over me, and I should have been leaving for church ten minutes earlier. I'm not a dirty person by nature, but I was covered in dirt at that moment—in more ways than one. What I needed was immediate personal hygiene to get the dirt off me so I could move on toward the plan already in place for the morning.

## Wash Off and Move On

In the same way, I encourage you not to think of yourself as a dirty person who can't be used by God. We all blow it at times, but that doesn't change the fact that, at the core of your being, you are clean because of what Christ has done for you. Maybe you need your feet to be washed off right now because you've been walking in the dirt.

Maybe you've even rolled down the hill. No big deal. Change clothes and move on toward the plan God has in place for you.

I'm not minimizing the seriousness of sin here. Nobody enjoys the aftereffect of a roll in the dirt. The point I'm making is, you don't have to let it wreck your life by believing you're a bad person God can't use. Your heart isn't wicked. You've been made clean—so don't think otherwise.

The Lord told Peter on another occasion, "What I've called clean, don't you call unclean" (see Acts 10:15). The same can be said to us about our hearts. You *used* to have a dirty heart, but not anymore. Christ has made you clean. In 1 Corinthians 6:9-11, Paul lists a number of kinds of unrighteous people, and then he goes on to say,

> Such *were* some of you; but you were washed, but you were
> sanctified, but you were justified in the name of the Lord
> Jesus Christ and in the Spirit of our God.

Don't cheat yourself out of the thrill of living in the carefree abandon of faith. Don't spend your life second-guessing yourself because you make the faulty assumption your heart can't be trusted. It can. You have the *Holy* Spirit putting His desires in your heart. For that reason, you can trust that He will guide you and keep your heart set on the path that is consistent with His will.

## What Do You Want?

Let's go back to our illustration of the person standing in the middle of the field, this time choosing to view it from a grace perspective. Some people, still motivated by fear, say, "I'll start by going in this direction. Pray for me, though. I'm going to take a step, but pray for me. I'm scared I'm going to miss the will of God. Pray for me that He'll protect me. O Lord, I'm going to go this way. Stop me. Please stop me if it's not right. Pray for me, friends." They move forward with a very tentative, timid, overcautious attitude.

That's not a grace walk. Grace reminds us that everything regarding our lives is God's responsibility. Again, the truth about knowing God's will is this: It's not up to you to find it. God will make His will known to you as you abide in Jesus Christ.

Some Christians think they have to "listen hard enough" to hear God. There it is one more time! Legalism, telling me what I must do. "I have to listen hard enough!" But grace takes the burden off me. Grace says, "You don't have to listen hard enough; God will speak *loudly enough.*" You can be sure of this—God is quite capable of speaking loudly enough to be heard.

> God...can speak loudly enough for you to hear Him. Don't worry that you're going to miss what He says.

When my children were growing up, if there was something I wanted one of them to do, I would communicate it to them. Let's say my son was watching TV. I would tell him, "I want you to go outside and cut the grass." But perhaps on this occasion, he's consumed with the program. I'd call his name: "Andrew." No—he's still consumed with his program. Again: "Andrew, I want you to cut the grass." He's still watching the TV. Finally I say more loudly, "Andrew!" "Yes, Dad?" he answers. "I want you to go out and cut the grass when your program is over." "Okay, Dad, I'll do it."

You see, the burden was on *me,* not him. He wasn't ignoring me or disrespecting me. The burden was on me to get his attention and communicate my desire. In grace, the burden is on God. He can speak loudly enough for you to hear Him. Don't worry that you're going to miss what He says.

*How* does God speak to us concerning His will? In our previous chapters we saw how God uses other Christians, circumstances, and the Bible to speak to us. Actually, there is no limit to the number of ways God can communicate with us.

But there is a way God commonly uses to speak to us that many

Christians don't recognize. God often speaks to us through our own desires.

## What Are the Desires of Your Heart?

In these next few pages I'd like to pull together several things we've been talking about. Consider this: If Jesus Christ can live His life through you, then He can also express His thoughts and desires through you. This can free you if you will let it. Remember what Paul said in 1 Corinthians 2:16: "We have the mind of Christ."

Now, consider this passage: "It is God who is at work in you, both to will and to work for His good pleasure" (Philippians 2:13). Look at the verse carefully. God is at work "to *will* and to *work*" according to His good pleasure. If He can *will* His pleasure, then God can create a desire in you. Did you know your desires can come from God? Have you ever considered that this is one way He can communicate His will to you, through your desires?

If you have a faulty conception of God, you might be one of those who say, "I'd really like to do this thing over here, but that can't be God's will—that would be too much fun. I would enjoy that. So God's will must be that miserable choice over there." That clearly reflects a false view of God.

On the other hand, have you discovered Psalm 37:4 for yourself? "Delight yourself in the LORD; and He will give you the desires of your heart." We touched on this verse briefly in chapter 5, but now let's spend some more time on it. Do you believe in a heavenly Father so good and kind that He *wants* to give us our hearts' desires?

As we honor our Lord, He places the desires in our hearts that He wants to be there and that He knows will bless us. Then He delights in meeting our deepest longings. As Jesus said,

> If you, then, being evil, know how to give good gifts to your children, how much more will your Father who is in heaven give what is good to those who ask Him! (Matthew 7:11).

## Let's Go Back to the Field

Remember the field? Imagine yourself again standing out in the middle of it, where you can see in all directions. This time, picture Jesus standing there with you. Jesus says to you, "There's a place I want you to go. Look around you." You see the beach over on one side, the mountain range on the other side, the meadow over there, the wooded forest opposite. Then Jesus says, "There's a place I want you to be."

"Where is it, Lord?" you ask.

"Look around," He says. "What interests you?"

"Wow," you reply. "I like the beach. I've always loved the ocean."

"You like that? There's a lot of territory in that direction. What about it do you like?"

"Well, I like that cluster of palm trees, and I like the hammock hanging there between those two trees that are reaching out toward the beach and the ocean."

"That's the place you like?" Jesus asks. "Then run to it. Take off—go! Run with all your might!"

Now picture yourself taking off, running with carefree abandon, as fast and furiously as you can toward the palm trees on the beach. And as you run and get closer, you see someone lying in that hammock. Then he stands up, and you can see that it's Jesus. There He is ahead of you, and He's shouting encouragement and laughing, "Come on! Run! Come to me! Run!"

You run to Him and to the place you've chosen. When you get there, Jesus throws His arms around you, sweeps you off your feet, and laughs as He spins you in a circle. "I'm glad you're here! I've been waiting for you."

He puts you down, and you say, "Jesus, how did You know?"

"How did I know what?"

"That of all the directions I could have gone, of all the places I could have picked, how did You know I'd come to this exact place?"

Jesus just looks at you and says, "Who do you think put the desire in you to come this way? Who do you think caused you to like the beach, or the meadow, or the woods? When you were choosing, who do you think led your thoughts and chose through you? I knew that palm tree and hammock would get you! The outcome of this wasn't you. It was all Me."

Do you get it? Do you understand how God's will can be accomplished in your life? It's not up to you to find and fulfill God's will for your life. Your only responsibility is to rest in Christ, and allow Him to be who He is in and through you.

## Trust Him, Then Decide

Jesus Christ will guide you. It's that straightforward. Don't complicate it, as we talked about in chapter 5. With that in mind, when you're faced with a decision, ask yourself these four simple questions:

1. "Am I trusting in Jesus Christ?"
2. "Is there one choice that would clearly increase my ability to share His life and His love with other people?"
3. "Am I willing to accept any outcome that God may will for me?"
4. "What do I want to do?"

Honestly answering these questions will help you to identify God's will in any situation. After that, there's only one thing left to do. Decide. Just decide. Jesus will stimulate your desires and think His thoughts through you. You have "put on Christ." That includes His mind. It's part of who you are. Be bold and act on your desires.

I'm not encouraging some sort of impulsive, shallow, feeling-based decision-making reaction. In a previous chapter I shared five checkpoints to use to make sure your decision-making lines up with God's Word and way. The tragic reality is, though, that for every Christian who makes a foolish or impulsive decision, there is another who will never make a decision for fear of failure.

Are you struggling over a decision? Maybe it's about what church to attend, which career path to follow, what university to attend, what house to buy, or something else. Don't make this hard on yourself. Have you prayed? Have you trusted Christ to guide you? Are you willing to do whatever He may want you to do? Then answer this question honestly: What do you *want* to do?

A good friend told me of having to make a decision related to the ministry he led. He kept praying for the Lord to make His will clear and tell him the choice He wanted him to make. He came down to the deadline, the zero hour where he had to decide. He kept praying repeatedly for God to tell him what to do.

He told me, "As I approached the deadline, finally I said, 'Lord, I'm desperate. What do you want me to do?' Finally the Lord spoke to me and said, 'I want you to *decide*.'"

This is an important thing for you to know! If you *know* who you are in Jesus Christ, if you know Christ *as your life,* you can trust His life within you. And an amazing thing about grace is that God trusts you to decide. After all, you two do live in *union* together.

Isn't that great? God trusts you to decide. What do you want to do? Do you want to run to the beach? Who do you think put that desire in you? You want that particular spot on the beach? Who do you think chose that spot through you? He will guide your thoughts.

Don't be paralyzed by analysis paralysis. Don't come to the place of no further progress in your grace walk because of your fear you might make a wrong choice. Do you want to know and do God's will? Then trust Jesus Christ. Recognize by faith that He is your life, and then... *decide!* And move forward in faith—not in apprehension and fear, but in faith—saying, "Lord God, thank You that You are my life. I will trust You to live through me."

Make your decisions on faith, not fear, and run boldly into them with confidence that Jesus will enable you to be in the center of His will as you practice the grace walk. You can trust your heart because of what your loving Father has done in it.

## ❊ G. R. A. C. E. GROUP QUESTIONS ❊

1. Briefly describe a time when analysis paralysis negatively affected your life. How does Psalm 56:3 apply to such moments in our lives?

2. Read Acts 16:6-7. What happened when the apostle Paul was about to make a wrong decision by going to a place God didn't intend for him to visit at that time? How does what happened in his life apply to your own life? Discuss an incident when the Spirit of Christ kept you from making a wrong decision.

3. The idea that our hearts are still deceitful and desperately wicked is prevalent in the modern church world. Discuss Ezekiel 36:26-27. When do we receive this new heart? Why can't the verse refer to the time when we get to heaven? (Hint—read 2 Peter 1:2-4.)

4. Compare 1 Corinthians 6:11 with Acts 10:15. What do you learn about how to see yourself from these two verses? How will believing the reality that we are clean in God's eyes empower us to follow our hearts in order to fulfill His will for us?

5. According to Psalm 37:4, what is the source of our desires as we trust in the Lord? How can we know that the flesh doesn't pollute our desires? If you were to follow your heart right now, where would it lead you?

### ~ Chapter 7

# Be Bold

Shortly before he died, the famous critic and playwright George Bernard Shaw was asked, "Mr. Shaw, if you could live your life over again and be anybody you know, or any person from history, who would you be?" Without hesitation, Shaw said, "I would choose to be the man George Bernard Shaw could have been, but never was."

All Christians have a desire to fulfill the plan God has for our lives. We don't want to reach the end of our earth-journey filled with regrets about what might have been.

Each of us has an allotted number of days to spend in this world, and once a day is past, it can never be reclaimed. How you spend the time you have in this world is an important matter. The psalmist prayed, "Teach us to number our days" (Psalm 90:12). Our days are a resource that can be spent to bring honor to God and great blessing to our lives and the lives of others.

As we mark the days on a calendar, looking forward to an event, we are also marking off the days behind. How do you want to spend each of your days? If they were money to be spent, how carefully would you contemplate spending each one?

God's plan for you is to lead you forward so you don't leave this world with a multitude of regrets. Christians have the potential to live the kind of life that will stand as an ongoing tribute to the goodness and grace of God. Our lives are to be a story that tells about His faithfulness and love.

## Living Above Regrets

For some of us, the challenge to be bold in the way we live is harder than it is for others. Life's circumstances can sometimes come at you with such violence and force that you're tempted to hunker down and give up the idea that there really is a God-sized plan for you that you could fulfill. Don't give in to that inclination. Your Father will bring you through the setbacks of your life and lead you onward. You may have suffered what seem to be major defeats along the journey toward the fulfillment of God's will for you. That doesn't mean you have failed.

Roger and Jan, who are friends of ours, faced a time when they wondered if their lives would be forever marred by a sense of regret. Roger was a successful salesman for a computer company. His career was moving along at a lively pace and life was good until a day came that changed everything. It was the day he discovered that the owner of the company, a professing Christian, had embezzled a million dollars. Corporate fallout was already starting. The owner was totally defiant about his actions.

> God's plan for their lives seemed to have run aground with no foreseeable way to recover.

In a moment, Roger knew God was telling him it was time to leave. The problem was, he was owed nearly $30,000. As he had suspected would happen, once he left, the owner refused to pay him.

Roger and Jan found themselves wondering what the will of God for their lives could possibly be. They had strongly believed that God's plan was to bless them through *this* job—and now it was all gone, with no options for gainful employment on the horizon.

In an attempt to resolve the matter, Roger asked his former employer if he would agree to Christian arbitration. The owner did, but when the process was complete and the mediator told him he had a biblical obligation to pay Roger what he was owed, the man sneered, "Who do you think you are to tell *me* what the Bible means?"

Roger and Jan struggled to make sense out of it all. God's plan for their lives seemed to have run aground with no foreseeable way to recover. There were restless nights as they tried to figure it all out…yet they sensed God assuring them He *did* have a plan and they simply needed to trust Him.

They agreed with each other that they would trust the Lord for their income. That commitment was tested, as no money at all came into their household for many months. They determined to keep trusting their Father, all the while wondering how He would work out bringing them the $30,000 they were owed. Then something happened that pushed their trust in God to the limit.

One night, as Roger lay awake in bed, he sensed God speaking to him. *"Forgive the debt,"* he heard in his mind. *Forgive the debt!* he thought. *Forgive the debt?* He knew he had a decision to make. Could good come from such a response? Could they trust God to that extreme?

Roger and Jan determined that they could. The next day Roger wrote his former employer a letter notifying him that the debt was forgiven. A few days later, he received a response from the owner's attorney. It was a release form that acknowledged Roger was formally and officially relinquishing any right to change his mind later about forgiving the debt. Roger signed the paper.

## Now What?

Now Roger and Jan had another decision to make. Would they live in regret about the past or look to the future in anticipation, believing that God still had a good plan for their lives? They chose the latter.

The thought came to Roger, *Maybe I could bring in a little income if I sold a computer to somebody. At least it would be something.* After all, that was one thing he had learned he could do. So he began to sell computers on his own, one here and one there. A few sales increased to more and more.

After a while, he reached the place where both he and Jan were needed to manage the growth of the company they had started. They just kept trusting God, believing He would lead them to fulfill the plan He had for them.

To say that He did would be an understatement. Today, 20 years later, Atlanta Computer Sales is not only a multimillion dollar company but also a testimony in the business world to God's goodness. It is an example of how our Father can redeem the failures of our lives and use them as stepping-stones toward the ultimate plan He has for us.

Maybe you also have had something happen to jar your confidence that God really does have a good plan for your life. Don't yield to your doubts. Determine to trust God anyway and live boldly. Don't assume that the ending to your story may be a gift with a bow on top, as with Roger and Jan, but remember this: *You don't know when you've reached the end of the story.* Only God does—and He can be trusted.

Whatever your failures and apparent setbacks of the past may be, don't lose hope. Trust your Father, who has promised to be with you always, all the way to the end. He will see to it that the plan He has for you is fulfilled. When you believe that fact, you will be empowered to live boldly instead of cowering in fear before the future.

The plan God has for your life was developed long ago. Your responsibility today is to trust Him and step up to the plate to assume your God-designed role. The Bible teaches that He wrote the script for all the days of your life before you lived a single one of them (see Psalm 139:16). Don't think for one minute that because life has had a serious downturn you've somehow lost out on living in the perfect will of God for your life.

Your destiny in time has already been established in eternity. The blueprint for your life exists in the eternal realm. You are known outside this world. A "cloud of witnesses" stands just beyond the veil, which separates time and eternity, and they encourage you onward and upward (see Hebrews 12:1).

## There's No Reason Not to Be Bold

When we recognize the reality of our God-given destiny, we discover boldness burgeoning inside us. Boldness was one of the main characteristics of those in the early church—and one of the most striking.

The book of Acts records how the believers were bold in preaching, praying, giving, worshipping, and evangelism. Many of them were even bold in the way they died. It appears they understood something that many Christians in the modern church either don't know or have forgotten. They knew that Christ was their Life. They knew that as they chose to depend on Him, He would animate all their thoughts and actions with divine power.

We need to grasp that same thing. In light of that understanding, why would anybody not want to live boldly? Daily experience, though, demonstrates that many of us do not.

However, your destiny is to boldly live a God-sized life and see some God-sized dreams realized. You aren't meant to simply shuffle through your existence here. Empowered by the indwelling Christ, you are capable of charging into life with the confidence you cannot fail. Because Christ is your life, you have in fact already succeeded, regardless of what unfolds in your circumstances. That truth provides the courage to follow the advice of the great missionary, William Carey, who said over two centuries ago, "Expect great things; attempt great things."

Grace not only equips us to be all we can be, but to do all we are called to do. Christians often live a listless lifestyle because, as I have noted, they either don't know or else don't believe that the actual power of Jesus Christ dwells within them. "You will receive power" was the promise of Christ to His disciples just before He ascended back to heaven (see Acts 1:8). Our lives are to be a witness to who He is as He lives His life through us in the person of His Spirit.

Your potential is unlimited because you have Unlimited Power living inside you. He has given you the abilities you possess. He is the one who will animate those abilities so you will accomplish more than you ever could otherwise.

You are destined for more than to loiter and languish on Planet Earth for 70 or 80 years and then go to heaven. This world isn't a waiting room. It is the stage upon which we live out the life of Christ in a way that is nothing short of supernatural. Every Christian's life is a unique expression of His infinite life and love.

## What Keeps Us from Living Boldly?

In an earlier chapter, we discussed how fear could cause us to live below the possibilities God has granted us. The default setting of unbelievers is one of fear—fear of failure, fear of rejection, fear of the world around them, and certainly fear of death (see Hebrews 2:14-15). They have fears about the economy, the marketplace, their job security, or the balance of their financial portfolio.

In contrast, the Bible teaches that Christians have every reason to be completely fearless in everything we do. Each of us has the right to be bold as a lion in every action of our lives, because the Lion of the tribe of Judah is our very life. People sometimes say, "It's a jungle out there," but the one who is our very life is King of the jungle!

Having dealt with our fears through His indwelling presence, Christ wants to move forward to eliminate other hindrances that will interfere with our being able to boldly live out His will for us.

A verse from the book of Proverbs puts its finger on another key problem that often keeps people from knowing and doing God's will with confidence. "The wicked flee when no one is pursuing, but the righteous are bold as a lion" (Proverbs 28:1). This proverb reveals another of the devil's favorite tactics to derail us. Why would someone flee "when no one is pursuing"? Because of another besetting human problem: *guilt*.

What does guilt have to do with knowing and doing God's will? Everything. A gnawing sense of guilt has caused people to cower and cringe before the challenges of life since the Garden of Eden. It was because of guilt that Adam and Eve hid from God after they sinned, despite the fact that He had created them to subdue and rule.

Guilt caused the king and queen of the world to shrink back behind a bush and try to hide themselves with fig leaves. Talk about forfeiting potential! But things haven't changed. It is because of guilt that people today still often cower in shame and uncertainty about what God's attitude toward them would be if they saw Him face-to-face.

Until we know how to address feelings of guilt, we run the risk of being paralyzed by it. Memories of the past can stand in our minds as perpetual monuments of our unacceptability to God. If you have been plagued by feelings of guilt, you probably have found it very hard to be motivated to believe that God has a wonderful plan in mind for you. Feelings of guilt can cause us to doubt God's love and acceptance of us in the present because of things we've done in the past.

## God's Answer for Guilt

Imagine for a moment that you had never done anything to feel guilty about. Wouldn't that be fantastic? What if any and every wrong thing you've ever done had never happened? Would that empower you to live boldly and confidently that God's plan is to bless you in all you do? Could you then move forward in pursuing God's will with boldness?

Grace brings that very news to you—news that seems almost too good to be true. It's this—your sins have been removed as if they never happened. They are *gone* and forgotten by God. When God looks at you, He sees you as if you have never sinned.

"How could that be?" you might ask. The answer is, it is possible because of what Jesus did when He came the first time. He dealt a death-blow to sin. Sin is not simply defeated; the blow against it through the cross *annihilated* it in your life. There is not even a trace of it left now.

Many of the prophets in the Old Testament predicted that a Messiah would come who would deal with sin once and for all. Daniel

spoke about Him and indicated that the
Christ would "make an end of sin" (Daniel
9:24). If you look that phrase up online in
a Hebrew lexicon (a reference source that
tells the meaning of the original words),
you will discover it means "to destroy or
finish." Jesus didn't come to just forgive
your sins. He came to obliterate them.

> ———⊰———
> When Jesus
> cried from the
> cross, "It is
> finished!" that's
> exactly what
> He meant.

When Jesus showed up at the Jordan
River, John the Baptist said about him,
"Look! It's the Lamb of God who has come
*to take away* the sins of the world!" (see John 1:29). What did John say
Jesus came to do? Forgive your sins? No, He does that, but it's even
better than that. He came to take them away completely.

When Jesus cried from the cross, "It is finished!" that's exactly what
He meant. Your sins were forever thrown away (see Hebrews 9:26)
behind the back of God (see Isaiah 38:17), wiped out (see Isaiah 44:22),
and forgotten (see Jeremiah 31:34). They will never be mentioned again
(see Hebrews 9:28)!

There is absolutely nothing now that would keep God from leading
you into the realization of the wonderful plan He has for your life.
Read the verses I've mentioned in the paragraph above and ask yourself,
"Are they true?" Did Christ really put away our sins by the sacrifice of
Himself, as Hebrews 9:26 says? If He came to *take away* our sins, did
He succeed or did He fail? Which was it? If He succeeded and our sins
are really gone, then why are we holding on to a guilty conscience?

## Leaving Guilt in the Past

I'll never forget the first time I met my friend Mike Quarles. I heard
him speak to a small group of ministry leaders. Mike's talk wasn't like
anything I had ever heard in such a meeting. He was telling the story of
his own journey toward fulfilling God's will for his life. The thing that
made his story unique to me was that he was being honest, *very* honest,
about some things most people would have skipped right past.

Mike had been a pastor for a number of years. He was a sincere man who wanted to make a difference in the world. As often happens with pastors, he reached a place where he began to become discouraged about his ministry. Discouragement turned to depression, and that depression finally led him to a major decision. He would leave the pastorate and return to the financial world, where he had been successful before as a stockbroker.

Mike's return to that kind of work afforded him the money benefits he had missed as a pastor. It didn't take long until he felt right at home back in the business culture. It was a stressful environment, but that's the way it is when your career is embedded in the stock market. Sometimes after work, Mike and his friends from work would stop by a bar to have a drink, just to relax and decompress from the stress of the day.

As time passed, Mike found himself drinking more and more. Gradually he became enslaved to alcohol. It became a serious problem for him, and his addiction began to impact him in every area of his life. His marriage began to unravel. "I became a falling-down drunk," he says today.

Ultimately, Mike's life fell to pieces because of his addiction to alcohol. His wife, Julia, made him leave. He spiraled downward further and further. In his attempt to get free from the grip his addiction had on him, Mike went through countless recovery programs. He met with people who were called "experts in spiritual warfare." He got counseling. He prayed. He begged.

Finally, after years of misery, Mike was set free when he came to understand who he is in Christ and what it means when the Bible teaches that believers are dead to sin and that it has no power over them. God restored his marriage and began to do a great healing work in every area of his life.*

None of this happened because of what Mike did, but because of what God did in him. It's only by trusting in Jesus Christ as our victory that we are free to live the way God designed. Mike puts it this way:

---

\* Adapted from Neil T. Anderson, Mike Quarles, and Julia Quarles, *Freedom from Addiction* (Ventura, CA: Gospel Light, 1996).

Pardon my Southern, but there are forty eleven dozen Christian programs and thousands and thousands of secular programs that will tell you what to do, *but* no one ever got saved, freed or sanctified by doing anything. No one ever will. Five hundred years ago Martin Luther said that nothing you *do* helps you spiritually. Only the truth will set you free (see John 8:32,36) and our response to the truth must be faith only.*

In the years since Mike was set free from his addiction, God has used him and his wife, Julia, greatly. They have coauthored (with Neil Anderson) *Freedom from Addiction,* a wonderful book that tells their story. They now work with the ministry I lead, teaching Grace Walk Recovery Conferences, where they help others learn how to live in freedom.

## *In Christ, Your Past Is* Past

Early on, Mike Quarles had to answer a question about his life. Would God use him after he had failed so miserably? Was there any hope he could ever again have a role in God's work?

The wonderful aspect of grace is that God's plan for our lives isn't set aside just because we make foolish choices. Maybe, like Mike, you've done some things that could cause you to think you will never be able to live out God's best plan for your life. Don't be deceived by that idea. God can use you *right now* if you will trust Him and move out in boldness. Your past is a part of your story, and your Father can use everything that has happened in your story to enrich the expression of His grace through you.

It is important for you to fully believe the truth that God has no grudge against you about your past that would keep Him from blessing you. Your past is forgiven. You are totally "bless-able" because your life is Christ, the One about whom the Father said, "This is my beloved Son, in whom I am well pleased!"

If I may be so bold, I want to shake you into reality by saying

---

* Steve McVey and Mike Quarles, untitled, unpublished manuscript, 2009

something that sounds harsh. Trust me—my intent is to help you. That's why I will speak so plainly. You've sinned? Welcome to the club. You have. Mike has. I have. We all have. It may look different in each of us, but sin has taken its toll on us all during our lives.

The good news of grace, though, is that Christ has dealt with your sin. It's history. So *get over it.* Until you get over it, you'll never be able to "get on with it," in regard to boldly living out the plan God has for you.

The truth is, your sins are forgotten. Now Christ within you wants to empower you to live boldly, with great expectations of what the Father has in mind for you. That's the truth—but it won't help you unless you *know* it's the truth. You've heard it said that "the truth will set you free," but that's not completely accurate. Jesus didn't say just that. What He said was, "*You shall know the truth* and the truth shall set you free."

The fact that Christ put away your sins is true. But you must *know* it to be true in order to experience freedom to move through life with boldness and peace about who you are and where you're headed. Will you affirm this truth right now? It's a sure way to take a big step toward experiencing God's will for you.

To live boldly, it is imperative to put a guilty conscience behind you. The sacrifice of Jesus Christ was enough for God. Is it enough for you? Surely you wouldn't set a standard higher than God Himself did, would you?

When we cling to self-condemning, guilty thoughts we are, in effect, insulting the finished work of Christ. We are saying to Him, "I know you died for me, but I need to help pay for my past by carrying guilt around with me from now on." Bad idea. Jesus said, "It is finished"—and it is. So let it go and begin to look toward the bright future your loving, gracious Father has in store for you.

Paul wrote regarding the past, "One thing I do: forgetting what lies behind and reaching forward to what lies ahead, I press on toward the goal for the prize of the upward call of God in Christ Jesus" (Philippians 3:13-14). Jesus said regarding the future, "Do not worry about tomorrow; for tomorrow will care for itself. Each day has enough trouble of its own" (Matthew 6:34). Therefore, live in this present moment. You can experience a carefree kind of life, knowing that God will care for you moment by moment.

## Embracing God's Purposes for Our Lives

You've now put your fears and guilt behind you. You thought you'd found security in the familiar, but you've realized your so-called security was really just a prison of doubt and fear that held you back from experiencing all that God wants you to enjoy. What now?

Some time ago, I was reading the Bible, and I noticed the words of Jesus in His final prayer before going to the cross.

> What you may feel emotionally isn't the criterion for measuring your boldness. It is actions that indicate boldness.

Although I had read these words many times before, it was as if I were seeing them for the first time. Tears filled my eyes as I read what Jesus said to His Father just hours before His crucifixion. "I glorified You on the earth, having accomplished the work which You have given me to do" (John 17:4).

I prayed that day, "Father, that's what I want to be able to say when I leave this world—that I've glorified You on the earth, and accomplished what You gave me to do."

While Christianity is not only about *doing,* we learn that as Christ lives through us, there certainly are things we will do during our lifetime to make an eternal difference. You obviously want to do those things He has planned for you, or you wouldn't be reading this book.

Though you were afraid to try new things, afraid of new situations, afraid of looking foolish to other people, afraid of failing if you were to try something different from your ordinary lifestyle, you are now beginning to move forward in faith. It's okay that you may think your faith is wobbly. Stepping out and moving forward is an act of boldness. What you may feel emotionally isn't the criterion for measuring your boldness. It is actions that indicate boldness. Faith, so to speak, is a verb, which points to action, not an adjective that describes feelings.

## Trust God in Every Circumstance of Life

Some people are afraid to live boldly because there was a time in their life when they took a risk by faith but things didn't turn out the way they expected. Years ago, one of my friends was very passive. He was very low-key in his approach to life, seemingly satisfied to just get by for one more day. One time he told me, "When I was a young man, I would take all kinds of chances."

"What changed?" I asked him.

"Well, when you get burned enough times, you become more careful about sticking your neck out," he replied.

"But have you ever considered that you might not be living up to your full potential?" I said.

Without hesitation he answered, "I know I'm not."

As we continued talking, I learned there had been a time in his life when he'd taken a real risk. He had stepped out in faith to take a new job he believed God was leading him to accept. Shortly after, the company had downsized. He was fired. Since that event years ago, he had tried to avoid taking another risk. He'd decided to play it safe.

### "Did I Make a Mistake?"

Like my friend, have you ever made a decision believing you were doing the will of God, only to have things turn out totally different from what you expected? Let's consider that. Go back in your mind to the imaginary scenario about the field I shared previously.

You were standing in an open field, with a 360-degree view. The different landscapes you saw represented different places you could go. Then we imagined Jesus asking which location you preferred. When you told him you like the beach with the palm trees and hammock,

He told you to run toward them. And when you arrived, there He was, waiting.

Now suppose you're lying in the hammock on the beach looking across the water. You notice a small cloud. Later, you look again and see that the cloud is a little bigger. You keep watching, and soon you see a storm brewing on the horizon.

Before you know it, that storm comes inland, and it's a hurricane. Now you find yourself holding on to one of those beautiful palm trees. Your feet are flapping behind you as the wind violently blows against you and you hang on for dear life.

You say in distress, "I thought the Lord led me here! How could this be happening to me? I thought this was the place God brought me to, but this isn't what I expected. I didn't know it would turn out like this. I must have missed His will."

Here again we can fall into a legalistic mind-set. We think we have missed God's will because things didn't turn out the way we expected. But if we understand the grace walk, we think differently. We don't assume we have missed God's will because things didn't turn out as we expected. Instead, we realize that God has a different agenda than the one we knew about, and He chose not to tell us our itinerary in advance.

Don't think you went wrong because you made a choice and things didn't come out the way you anticipated. That doesn't mean you missed God's will. Consider these questions: "Were you trusting Christ? Were you depending on Him? Were you willing to do whatever the Lord led you to do? Did you want His will? Is Jesus Christ your life? Is God sovereign?" If the answers to those questions are "Yes," then God's will has been done in your life, even though it didn't turn out the way you anticipated.

Don't stay in a place where you live with the play-it-safe mind-set. Your God has great plans for you! Grace Murray Hopper, a navy admiral in the last century, once said, "A ship in port is safe. But that's not what ships are built for." We were not made for "safety" as our highest value. We were made to live an adventure!

## Trust That God Remains in Control

Even Christ's apostles experienced the unexpected. Paul decided it was God's will for him to go to Rome and preach the gospel. He mentions this frequently in his letters as a deep desire. Things didn't turn out exactly the way he had planned. En route, he found himself shipwrecked on the island of Malta, hundreds of miles from his destination. Unforeseen by the apostle, God decided that, before Paul got to Rome, this shipwreck would occur and Paul would find himself sharing the gospel with the inhabitants of the island.

Now, Paul might have moaned, "I missed the will of God," but he knew better. God just had a different plan than he had informed Paul about!

Or take the apostle John. He knew it was God's will for him that he preach the gospel. He might have assumed he was to preach the gospel for life. But God determined that John would be exiled to an island called Patmos. Why? So he could write the book of the Revelation. John had a plan, but God had a different plan he didn't tell John in advance.

In my book *Grace Walk*, I tell the story of how I moved to Atlanta, Georgia, in 1990, thinking it was God's will for me to go there to build "a great church." God did lead me to Atlanta, but it wasn't so I could build a great church. The Lord didn't tell me in advance why He was really taking me there. His plan was bigger than mine. He was taking me to Atlanta to allow me to experience brokenness, and to teach me my identity in Christ.

If you're interested, you can read the whole story in *Grace Walk*. What I want you to see now is this: God's will *is* going to be done in your life. Just because things didn't turn out the way you anticipated, don't think you've missed it. Don't beat yourself up over it.

What disappointments have you experienced in life? Have you been taken captive by the lie that, because you've made a wrong choice, you are doomed to settle for less than God's perfect will for your life? Let me reassure you that God is big enough to make sure His will is accomplished!

Someone else might lament, "But I've sinned! And that sin has had unchangeable effects on my life—unchangeable consequences that will always prevent God's perfect will from coming true for me."

If that is your question, I want to ask you, "Do you believe God is omniscient? Do you believe He knows everything about everything?" Before you were even born, He knew every decision you would make in your whole lifetime. Your decisions may have surprised and disappointed *you,* but they didn't surprise God. He knew them all along.

## Was God Taken by Surprise?

You're not going to get to heaven and hear God say, "Well, I had planned to do this in your life...but I didn't expect you to go and make *that* bad choice." No. God's not going to say that. He *knows.* He knows every choice you're ever going to make, and He is able to work out His plan in your life. *Trust Him*—regardless of where you are today. You might truly have made a major mess of things, possibly created your own personal hell. But God will never tell you, "Well, you made your bed...now lie in it." He's going to say, "I'm here, and I'll lead you *from right here where you are* into the perfect plan I have for your life."

The psalmist said,

> Where can I go from Your Spirit?
>     Or where can I flee from Your presence?
>         If I ascend to heaven, You are there;
>     If I make my bed in Sheol, behold, You are there.
>         If I take the wings of the dawn,
>             If I dwell in the remotest part of the sea,
>     Even there Your hand will lead me,
>         And Your right hand will lay hold of me.
>                 —Psalm 139:7-9

Note that David even said, "If I make my bed in Sheol"—Hebrew for the grave, the realm of the dead—"behold, You are there." Somebody may say, "But I've created my own living hell. I may as well be dead. How can I possibly be in the center of God's will?" How? Because God's there *with you* in the hell you created. Trust Him! He will lead you out and guide you. Believing this fact will give you the confidence to live boldly in the center of His will. Wherever He is, there we will find our center.

If knowing the truth sets you free, then believing lies will hold you in bondage. Don't believe the lie that you'll never be able to experience God's best for your life because of wrong choices you've made. Trust Him instead. Trust Him in every circumstance of life.

### He's Bigger Than Our Foolishness

"But I made a decision while *not* trusting in the Lord," says another person. "My decision and motivation came out of the flesh and sin. How could I be in the center of God's will?" I want to say it again, before you were ever born, God saw everything from start to finish. He saw every decision you were ever going to make—the right ones and wrong ones—the good ones and bad ones. He saw all of them.

Based on His sovereign decrees, every decision you were going to make in your lifetime was incorporated into the master plan. I believe that when we get to heaven, we'll look back at some of the dark threads in the tapestry of our lives, some of those times when we made foolish decisions, and we'll see that those dark threads fit seamlessly and perfectly into the beautiful pattern of God's story for us.

> The God we serve is…bigger than our stupidity. I'm glad for that, aren't you?

No, He didn't cause us to make those sin-generated, flesh-oriented decisions. But the great thing about the God we serve is that He's bigger than our stupidity. I'm glad for that, aren't you? I've made some foolish choices in my life, but God is bigger than our foolishness.

Knowing everything about you, and knowing every decision you would make, He orchestrated it all to accomplish His purpose in your life. You're never going to jump the tracks so far that you'll miss His will. Turn to Him and trust Him. Take hold of the great adventure before you, and live boldly by faith in Jesus Christ.

## ❋ G.R.A.C.E. GROUP QUESTIONS ❋

1. What is the greatest setback you have experienced in your lifetime? How has God's grace empowered you to move beyond it and see His plan fulfilled in your life to this point? Or have you "stalled out"? Read 2 Corinthians 11:25-30 and 2 Corinthians 12:10. How did the apostle Paul view his setbacks?

2. Read Proverbs 28:1 and discuss areas of your life where you can apply its truth. What specific actions will you take to exercise boldness in these areas?

3. Put Hebrews 9:24-28 in your own words. What did Christ do regarding your sins? What difference does believing that fact have on feelings of guilt about your past?

4. Name three people in Scripture who made horribly foolish choices and yet went on to be mightily used by God. (If you have any trouble with this question, look at Hebrews 11.) Pray and tell the Lord you know that your sins are forgiven and that He plans to use your life.

5. When is a time in your life when you believed that you were out of God's will? Looking back on it now, how did God use that time in your life? In what ways can you recognize now that He was moving you forward according to His plan even though you didn't see it at the time? (Psalm 139:7-9 applies here.)

# CHAPTER EIGHT

# Be Yourself

COMING TO THE END OF THIS BOOK presents you with a choice. One option is to just close the book, having treated it like many books you've been exposed to along the way in your journey of faith. Sometimes we enjoy books we read. (Since you didn't stop reading before reaching this last chapter, I assume that much.) We may even feel we've gained some insight from them. Then we set them aside and go on with life as usual. You could do that.

There are other times, though, that it's different. We somehow sense deep within us that something has shifted. We realize we haven't just read a book, but the book has read us. It touched us at places in our lives that needed to be healed by truth, and we sense that the healing has begun. In those instances, we don't just put the book down and go on in the same way. We choose to integrate what God has shown us into the way we think and act.

I hope that is the case as you end this book. The last page of this chapter can be a gateway to the beginning of a new way of life in your personal grace walk. No book has inherent power to transform lives, but sometimes the Holy Spirit does take what somebody has said and apply it to our lives so that we recognize His Voice behind the lesser voice.

I don't have it all together in my own life at times. Sometimes I tell my wife, Melanie, "I don't understand this stuff. I just teach it!" At those times I'm being ironic, of course. The point I'm making is that the treasure is most definitely in an "earthen vessel." But having admitted that, I can tell you that understanding the things I've written in this book have transformed my life. Grace has a way of doing that to a person, no matter whether the subject is knowing God's will or anything else.

As you finish, it is important to decide how you are going to respond. Will you close this book and go on living the way you have in the past? Or will you allow the things the Holy Spirit has taught you to set a new course for you, so you can move ahead with new understanding and a new approach to confidently living in God's will each day?

Maybe walking in the will of God as I've described in this book sounds too easy to you. If so, I suspect the reason it seems that way is because you've been taught an approach that may be laced with legalism. However, doesn't it make sense that a God of grace *would* make it easy to know His will? Isn't that what grace is all about? Why in the world would He want to make it next to impossible to be sure of His will and then confidently do it? To embrace a new understanding of His will may require a change. It may mean moving from a legalistic mind-set to a view through the lens of grace.

Living things always change. Are you willing to be changed by applying the truth of God's Word that you've read here? You can be sure that God's plan for you is that your best days are still ahead. He always leads us "from glory to glory."

There is no negative aspect of your life that is bigger than the ability God has given you. This is the ability to take whatever days you have left in this world and make them the days of the greatest impact you will have in your lifetime. The climax of your God-given destiny lies ahead of you, not behind you.

Own these truths. Assimilate them into every fiber of your perception of God, yourself, and the world around you. Don't listen to anything you hear from within or without that would suggest otherwise.

## Do You Want to Walk?

Sometimes a person's view of life has calcified to the point that their dreams and hopes have become completely stagnant. They think that the days ahead will be no different than the days behind. They still breathe, but in many ways they died a long time ago.

Jesus met a man like that one day. The fifth chapter of John tells the story of an afflicted man whom Jesus encountered. This particular man had been paralyzed for 38 years. As he lay by the Pool of Bethesda, he watched other people see their dreams come true. Every now and then, an angel would come and stir the water in the pool. Immediately afterward, the first one who got into the pool would be healed of whatever problem he had.

One day Jesus came to that pool and saw the man lying there. "Do you want to get well?" Jesus asked him. "I can't get into the water and nobody will help me," the man answered. Jesus said to the man, "Get up, take your mattress and walk." Immediately the man did what Christ said. He simply got up and walked away (see John 5:1-9).

Before the paralyzed man was healed, he had to come face-to-face with a question that seems almost bizarre on the surface. "Do you want to get well?" Jesus asked him. "Do I *want* to get well?" the man might have asked. "What kind of question is that? Of course I want to get well!"

That's not what he said, though. Instead he began to explain why being well was outside the realm of possibility for him. Somewhere along the way, his dream of ever walking again had died. Jesus, however, is in the business of resurrecting things that have died. With loving compassion, He simply said to the man, "Get up." Inherent in His word was both the motivation and the ability for the man to finally do what his heart had yearned to do for years—to walk.

What dreams lie dormant inside your heart that were once alive and vibrant? It is important for you to realize that those dreams may be the voice of God within you nudging you toward rising up and fulfilling

His plan for your life. What would you do if Jesus said to you today, "Get up and do it"? How long have you watched other people's dreams come true while you lay on the sidelines?

### Your Best Choice Now

Abby FitzPatrick is one of my heroes. The thing you may find surprising is that she is only 11 years old. Abby has a rare illness called mitochondrial disease. Mitochondria are the powerhouses of nearly every cell in our bodies, and they are responsible for converting substances from the foods we eat into energy for essential cell functions. The cell functions in turn run all of the organs and systems in our bodies. The process of converting food into that energy requires hundreds of chemical reactions, and every one of them has to run almost perfectly in order for us to have a continuous supply of energy. When one or more components of these chemical reactions don't run perfectly, there is an energy crisis, and the cells can't function normally. As a result, there is not enough cellular energy to run the essential systems in the body—such as the heart, liver, kidneys, digestive tract, muscles, and brain.

> Don't let yourself get bogged down by your circumstances. They don't define you.

Mitochondrial disease is serious, to say the least. Nonetheless, Abby is an amazing girl, animated by divine power. She is in the Beta Club organization. As her energy allows, she swims and runs and plays like all 11-year-old girls. This year she was on the volleyball team at the local YMCA. She knows how serious her health problem is, but she has decided to live every day to the fullest degree possible.

Sometimes when I'm dealing with the routine frustrations of life, I think about Abby. I wonder what kind of day she has had. I'm reminded of how she handles the hard days and I think to myself, *Life is too short to sit on the sidelines. If Abby can run the race with gusto, despite her challenges, I have no excuses.* So I shake off my petty attitude and determine to move ahead with faith and hope.

Are there any good excuses you have for not running the race with gusto? You've had some debilitating things happen in life? Okay, so what are you going to do now? You may think your situation is "sick," but you have divine life pulsing through you. It's who you are. Don't let yourself get bogged down by your circumstances. They don't define you. Your Creator has defined who you are, and He says that you have been created as somebody who is filled with divine potential.

### Think—Do You Want to Be Well?

Maybe you've been set on the sidelines, seemingly handicapped by life's circumstances. Here's the question you must answer: Do you want to be well? Some people don't. To be well means they would have all their excuses taken away from them and they wouldn't be able to blame their circumstances anymore. They could no longer say other people were at fault.

To be well, they would have to assume full responsibility for getting up and stepping out in faith to do God's will. It would be them and Jesus. They wouldn't be able to play the role of a victim anymore. No more excuses. No more delays. *Do you want to be well?*

You can be well. God's will is most definitely for you to know and believe this fact: *It's your turn! Your day has come!* Jesus is speaking to you right now. Deep inside you something is stirring. It is a hope that all this might be true.

Well, it is. Your day has come because God is faithful to His promises. "Strength for today, and bright hope for tomorrow, blessings all mine, with ten thousand beside!" wrote hymn-writer Thomas Chisholm. If you will believe in your Father's goodness and in His desire to lead you into fulfilling His will, your life can change. Will you appropriate the ability to fulfill God's will for your life because of what Jesus has done?

Maybe something inside you needs to change if you are going to "get up and walk." The longer you have lain on the sidelines and meditated on your own pitiful condition while others walked onward, the more necessary it is for you to change the way you think. Sometimes you need to recover what you know to be true.

Do you want to realize the wonderful potential that God has planned for you? He will enable you to get up and go. The paralytic had been beside that pool for 38 years. Years before Jesus came to him, he had probably reached the point where his thoughts about the future were shaped by his circumstances in the past. He had imagined every conceivable scenario as to how he might walk—and none of them had seemed viable. At some point, the dream inside him had died.

There was, however, one thing he hadn't imagined. It had never crossed his mind that maybe one day the Son of God Himself would come in person and raise him up. But Jesus did. That was a possibility that was simply beyond the paralytic's frame of reference.

Did you know that God is irresistibly drawn to impossible situations? He loves to show up at times when things seem hopeless. His style is to wait until all hope is gone and then burst onto the scene with a gush of grace. That's why you should never give up hope in Him. He's the God of good surprises.

## Just Step Out

In chapter 4 I told you part of the story about when the Lord led me to leave the pastorate and start an itinerant ministry. It was definitely scary. Melanie and I prayed about it separately and together. We had to be sure. The thought of stepping out of what we thought was the security of my position as pastor of our church was terrifying. If we did it, we would have to accept the fact that we didn't know how we would get an income to live.

The enemy described in my imagination what it would look like when the mortgage company foreclosed on our house and the sheriff's department set all our furniture on the side of the road. I could imagine myself standing at the side of a busy intersection holding a sign that said, "Will Preach for Food." Okay, maybe it wasn't that bad, but I did find myself thinking irrational thoughts at times. Fear can attack you that way.

I remember the night Melanie and I got a babysitter for the kids and went off alone. We drove up to a lodge north of Atlanta where we could be alone and quiet. We prayed that night, seeking to be sure about God's will for us. After praying and talking most of the night, we left there having decided that we were going to leave our comfort zone and launch out into what we believed God was unfolding for us.

Since then, the results have been miraculous. I've had the opportunity to travel the world sharing God's grace with people. I've preached in a leper colony in India. I've smuggled Bibles into a Communist country. I spoke of God's grace to an influential leader of a movement down in southern Mexico, a man who is responsible for the martyrdom of Christians. A few years ago, I secretly visited a rural part of a country where it is illegal for Christians to even meet together. I was completely hidden from head to toe and traveled under the cloak of darkness in order to teach and encourage leaders of the underground church there. Those leaders risked years in prison to hear more about God's Word and to become better equipped to serve.

I've stood on the borderline of the DMZ between South Korea and North Korea. I have traveled to Japan, China, England, Norway, and the Netherlands. I've shared this message all over Latin America. In Africa, I spoke to children orphaned by the AIDS pandemic and to leaders who have come to understand that the hope for that continent is the message of Christ as life. Grace Walk Ministries has now opened offices in numerous countries, and ministry opportunities are still wide open in other places around the world.

## God Is Delighted to Use Anyone

Why have I told you all this? Certainly not to try to impress you. To the contrary, I'm making the point that *God will use anybody.* That includes you.

You don't have to be a superstar to experience great things from God. We were afraid to do what we did, but now I thank God that

He moved us forward despite our fears. I'm just a regular guy who served as pastor of medium-sized churches for over 20 years—but then God spoke to me, revealing this grace walk to me, inviting me to join Him in this exciting adventure of experiencing Christ living through me.

If He did that in my life, He'll do it in yours. The plan He has for you won't be the same one He has for me. It'll be better for you than the plan He has for me, because God's plan for you will be custom-made. It will fit your gifts, your personality, and your style.

It is never too late to experience His will. God can do more, in one day, living through you, than you could accomplish in a lifetime on your own. Now that is good news!

God is calling you to live in His will, which is to consciously live in union with Him through Jesus Christ. God will act in this world through you. That's His will for you. He's calling you to this exciting adventure I call the grace walk.

In the grace walk, we don't have to conjure up our own plan. We don't have to figure out the will of God. We don't have to find it, as if it were hidden somewhere out in the cosmos. The grace walk is our God revealing to us, through the Person of Christ, His will for us day by day. It is Jesus Christ living through us.

That's His will for you. Will you join Him in what He's doing? Don't worry about how it will all come about. Let your eyes be open to "the surpassing greatness of His power toward us who believe" (Ephesians 1:19).

## Don't Expect God to Work Within Your Expectations

Don't worry about obstacles you may face. Whatever your lifestyle might be right now, remember this—things can suddenly change for you. In a moment, life can turn around. Don't think that your life will always be like it is now. God can change things for you. Believe Him for His blessings. Never give up on Him. God indeed does love you and have a wonderful plan for your life.

Maybe you've lived life on the same track for many years. You've thought about your dreams, but they have seemed impossible. After all, considering your circumstances, how could things be different?

Don't judge your future by your past, as I've said before. If you sense that God's will for you requires a change, know that it can happen, and start to move toward it. Change will come. It might be today. If not today, it might be tomorrow. Keep persevering and trusting God because He is good and certainly deserves your trust.

God often chooses to act in our lives outside the way we think He will work. Just because you've seen Him work in other's lives in a particular way doesn't mean that is the way He'll work things out for you. Stop comparing yourself to other people. Don't look for your plan to materialize in a certain way. Give up your preconceived expectations. Only look to Jesus. He will resolve the problem in the way He wants, not necessarily in the way you anticipate.

Like the paralyzed man, you might look up at any moment and see Him standing beside you, inviting you to get up and realize your life purpose in this world. Things will change. You can count on it. It may not work out the way you expect or even want right now, but He will call you up and out from your afflicted condition. He will equip you to fulfill the plan He has for your life. He will do it.

Are you willing to experience life in new, unfamiliar ways? Are you willing to step up and out in faith? It may seem scary, but just trust Him, and then trust Him some more!

## Change the Station

Some people have a negativity broadcast going on inside them practically all the time. Sometimes it is conscious; at other times it is subconscious. This negativity causes them to look at a scenario and immediately see the bad aspects of it.

"Do you want to get well?" Jesus asks them. But they don't even hear the question. Like the man beside the pool, their response is immediately a negative, "why it won't work for me" one.

They are prophets of doom for themselves. "I've always been this way." "It's just the way I am." "That could never work because..." "My situation is different." They have a thousand reasons why things won't change for them. They will say they wish things could change, but then torpedo their own desires by reminding themselves of all the reasons why things never will.

This negativity broadcast will deeply affect any of us if we don't change stations. Here's how it happens: As the discordant background "music" plays in our minds, it creates a certain mood within us. That mood influences the way we think about things. Together, the way a person thinks and feels creates a certain inner paradigm for life—a negative one.

> What is the attitude you have toward challenges in your life?

This negative paradigm determines our expectations when we face any situation—and those expectations are nothing less than a reflection of our faith. Jesus said, "According to your faith, so be it unto you." It becomes clear, then, from the results we get, that some of us are going through life exercising great faith—*negative* faith! Then we wonder why things don't seem to "go our way." *According to your faith be it unto you.*

What is the attitude you have toward challenges in your life? Some years ago I read the story of the late Sir Edmund Hillary, the first Westerner to climb Mount Everest. Of all the possible people to gain this distinction, Hillary was an unlikely candidate. He had lived a simple life as a beekeeper in Auckland, New Zealand. But deep inside him was an idea most people would have considered ridiculous. He wanted to climb the mountain.

Reaching his goal wasn't something that came without its challenges. In 1952 he made an attempt but failed to reach the top. His response to that failure is what set him apart from others.

A few weeks after his failed attempt, a group in England asked Hillary to speak to their members. When he walked onto the stage, they greeted him with cheers and thunderous applause. They obviously recognized the value of the attempt he had made, but he didn't see it that way. He wasn't content to stop at the place of seeing his goal almost realized.

Walking over to one side of the platform, he pointed to a picture of Mount Everest hanging on the wall. Then he clenched his fist and loudly cried out, "Mount Everest, you beat me the first time, but I'll beat you next time because you've grown all you're ever going to grow, but I'm still growing!" And on May 29, 1953, along with his partner, Tenzing Norgay, he accomplished his goal, scaling to the top at 29,000 feet.

Edmund Hillary had tapped into a truth we all need to understand. *Where we are today doesn't have to be the final word on where we will be in the end.* God does have a plan for your life, and He will fulfill it in you. Do you believe that? Are you still growing in faith—or have you resigned yourself to the lie that reaching the mountaintops in life is beyond your potential? Understand that your mountaintop is nothing more or less than fulfilling the plan God has for you.

### Has Unbelief Got You in a Box?

Why did Israel wander in the wilderness for 40 years? It was because of their negative faith. The Bible says, "They were not able to enter because of unbelief" (Hebrews 3:19). Too many people have blamed God, other people, or just their own "bad luck" for not reaching their destiny. But the truth is, the fault lies squarely in their own refusal to believe in God's basic goodness and in His desire to guide them in fulfilling His will. If you are waiting for God to act, has it occurred to you that God may be waiting for *you?*

Put any of us in any situation and we will begin to draw conclusions based on what we see. We will evaluate our situation and mentally predict how things are going to unfold. In other words, we will come to *believe* that we know what our future will hold.

Those beliefs become our faith system. Once it is established, it becomes very hard to think outside the walls of expectations we have built around ourselves. We box ourselves in by our limited thinking, which developed through our own very human assessment of our life situation at a certain moment in time. Functioning now from a limited negative faith, we begin to look for evidence in our circumstances that validates our initial analysis. "See, I knew it!" we cry when visible evidence seems to support our negative perspective.

The box closes in on us as we affirm again and again that "this is just the way things are" and as we appropriate hopelessness over things ever changing. Our faith…our *negative* faith…grows by leaps and bounds. Every day seems to take us further away from hope.

Now, I've heard people say we shouldn't put God in a box. "Let Him out of the box!" they'll challenge others. Let me tell you something: It's not God who is in the box. It's *us*. God is too big and too powerful to be boxed in by our puny negative faith.

Instead, our Father of grace appeals to us, "Come out of your box and believe Me, and I'll do great and mighty things like you can't imagine" (see Jeremiah 33:3).

Begin to expect things to go your way because God is "for you." (And begin to expect your way to become His way as He shapes your desires.) Recognize that God's grace equals guaranteed success. Approach life with an optimistic expectancy based on the goodness of God.

God once told Abraham, "I will give you the land as far as you can see." There is a relevant principle embedded in that promise, which raises a question: What can *you* see? Do you see life never advancing, never expanding? Maybe the only thing that needs to change for you to move boldly into the fulfillment of your potential is your focus, the "broadcast" you're tuned into.

Have you been paralyzing your life by appropriating negative outcomes in the situations you face? Is there an AM (awful mentality) station playing in the background inside your head all the time? Change stations to FM (faith mentality)!

## A Reminder—It Is His Plan, and He Will Fulfill It

As you get out of your faith box, you'll begin to see the truth I've been building on throughout this book. Your heavenly Father has a plan for you—and it isn't up to you to fulfill it. You are simply to walk the path He sets before you, zealously working toward the fulfillment of your dreams in the power of His Spirit. As you do, He causes your dreams and abilities to grow and fulfills His will for you. He already has it all worked out—the plan, the process, and the results.

Isaiah said to God in prayer, "You have worked wonders, plans formed long ago, with perfect faithfulness" (Isaiah 25:1). We can just relax and move ahead because He has already accomplished in eternity the good things we will experience in time. Isaiah also said, "LORD, You will establish peace for us, since you have also performed for us all our works" (Isaiah 26:12). Not only does our Father plan the work, He works the plan! Can you see that it's a done deal?

The apostle Paul zeros in on this aspect of the Christian's life mission in Ephesians 2:10. I love the way the verse is rendered in *The New Living Translation:*

> We are God's masterpiece. He has created us anew in Christ Jesus, so that we can do the good things he planned for us long ago.

Some say that Paul may be the most effective Christian who ever lived. If a man ever fulfilled God's will for his life, it was Paul. In speaking about the fulfillment of his own God-given goals, here's how he described his success: "For this purpose also I labor, striving according to His power, which mightily works within me" (Colossians 1:29). In another place, he wrote,

> By the grace of God, I am what I am, and His grace toward me did not prove vain; but I labored even more than all of them, yet not I, but the grace of God with me (1 Corinthians 15:10).

Do you see Paul's secret of effectiveness? He said, "I work. Yes, I work hard, but it isn't by *my* power. It is *His* power that is at work in me. It is His *grace* that causes me to be effective."

## Do You Expect God to Be Good to You?

The foundation for your optimism (and Paul's) about knowing and doing God's will is Jesus Christ. Faith in Him is the conduit through which He is able to pour out into your life all the good He has planned for you to be, to have, and to do. That fact again raises a question of faith: Do you believe that God wants you to experience and enjoy His blessings or not? As you look down the path that lies ahead for you, do you anticipate good things from God? Do you expect things to become better or worse?

Will you choose to believe what God says about it? He declares that "the path of the righteous is like the light of dawn, that shines brighter and brighter until the full day" (Proverbs 4:18). Since you have been made righteous by Jesus Christ (see Romans 5:17 and 2 Corinthians 5:21), this promise is directed toward you.

Combine the promises of God with His ability and faithfulness to keep those promises, and there is no reason to be anything but positive!

> Be strong and courageous,
> all you who put your hope in the Lord.
>
> —Psalm 31:24 NLT

> The Lord's delight is in those…
> who put their hope in his unfailing love.
>
> —Psalm 147:11 NLT

> There is surely a future hope for you,
> and your hope will not be cut off.
>
> —Proverbs 23:18 NIV

Will you lay hold of the hope of fulfilling the God-given dreams of your heart? The apostle Paul did. He wrote triumphantly, "Now all glory to God, who is able, through his mighty power at work within us, to accomplish infinitely more than we might ask or think"

(Ephesians 3:20 NLT). And the writer of Hebrews tells us, "Let us hold tightly without wavering to the hope we affirm, for God can be trusted to keep his promise" (Hebrews 10:23 NLT).

## God's Will for You Is a God-Sized Plan

Several years ago, a man won the big jackpot of the Georgia state lottery. Immediately, this man of humble means became a millionaire. I remember a reporter asking him on the news, "What do you plan to do now that you've won the multimillion-dollar jackpot?"

The man's answer reflected the limited paradigm of how he had lived for so many years. After a few seconds of thought, the man replied, "I'm going to buy me a double-wide trailer and move to Alabama."

His answer struck me as funny. This was the best thing he could think of to do with his new millions. However, in another way it struck me as sad. Although there is nothing wrong with living in a double-wide mobile home with millions of dollars at your disposal, this was as high as the man's imagination could go.

> May God...use your humanity, freely yielded to Him, to accomplish great things for His glory.

I believe there are many Christians who, though they share the life of Christ and serve an omnipotent God, have a "double-wide trailer" mentality. They think that if they can just get by in life and then go to heaven when they die, everything's going to be okay.

If that's your mind-set, I encourage you to break free from it. Don't be held captive by small thoughts. You belong to a great God, who wants to use your life in great ways! I don't necessarily mean ways that are great according to the measuring stick of the world. I'm talking about greatness as *He* defines it.

What is it that you would be thrilled to see Jesus Christ do in and through you? Maybe it's to advance your education or make a career change. Maybe it's finding the courage to marry. Maybe it's to start a ministry. Maybe it's to be the means of transformation in people you think will never change. Maybe it's to take what you're already doing to a higher level.

God is inviting you to join Him in accomplishing His will in this world. Will you do it? Will you join together with Christ, understanding your union with Him? Will you tell Him, "Lord Jesus, I want you to live through me"?

Stop worrying about God's will—that you're going to miss it. Just rest. Relax. Recall again that it's not up to you to figure it out. Just focus on Jesus Christ, and understand that He is your life. Remember— as you focus on Him and abide in Him, you can trust Him to live through you, think through you, and accomplish His will through you.

May God do great things for and through you. May He use your humanity, freely yielded to Him, to accomplish great things for His glory, for which you will thank Him throughout eternity. May you live the adventure with joy and hope as you experience the grace and the freedom of walking in the will of God.

## ❀ G.R.A.C.E. GROUP QUESTIONS ❀

1. What is the most important lesson you have learned from this book? What biblical truth do you understand differently now than you did before you read the book? What difference will this new understanding make in your life in regard to walking in God's will?

2. Compare Proverbs 13:15 with Matthew 11:30. In what ways have many Christians made it seem hard to find God's will for their lives? Explain how a grace-based way of understanding God's will for your life is easy.

3. Jesus asked the man in John 5, "Do you want to be well?" What are some common reasons why people don't really want to move beyond the obstacles that prevent them from enjoying the grace and freedom of walking in the will of God? What excuse have you used in the past about not moving forward in your own life? What will be different now as a result of what God has shown you?

4. Is there an area in your life where you sense that the best choice would be to step out in faith? What is that area, and what do you plan to do to move forward toward walking in His will for your life in it?

5. In what ways have you allowed an AM (awful mentality) broadcast to play in the background of your mind? How do you plan to change to an FM (faith mentality) broadcast now? What changes will occur in the way you choose to think about your circumstances and to act?

6. Read Jeremiah 33:3 and respond to it through a prayer.

# A Final Word

SUSANNAH WAS A YOUNG GIRL WHO PRAYED the same prayer every day: "Dear God, guide me. Help me to do your will. Make my life count." It seemed like the only answer she got was "Wait."

Eventually she got married, still wondering why God hadn't launched her toward fulfilling the great plan for her life she longed to see unfold. Then her children began to be born. As a devout Christian mother, Susannah taught her children the faith that guided her own life.

When she died years later, Susannah hadn't done the things she had envisioned as a young girl. She had never written a book. She had never spoken in church. She had never become a missionary.

Did she fulfill God's will for her life? The answer rests in the fact that although she died in 1742, what she did still has impact today. If you have ever sung "Christ the Lord Is Risen Today" or "Hark, the Herald Angels Sing" or one of hundreds of other hymns, you've sung songs written by Susannah's son Charles Wesley. Another of her sons, John, would establish Methodism, a movement that has given birth to thousands of local churches around the world.

Susannah Wesley prayed to know and do God's will, but during her lifetime she might have questioned how much impact she was having in this world. Rearing children hardly seemed to be the kind of world-changing endeavor she had dreamed about as a young girl, but it was.

❧❧

What are you doing with your life? Don't underestimate how God may use you in your daily walk as you stay focused on Him and what He has put right in front of you. As you stay focused on Jesus Christ as the source of your life, God will use you to make a difference in ways you may not fully realize.

I have written this book with the hope that it would both encourage and instruct you about how to know and carry out the plan God has for your life. As I have noted throughout, this whole topic has often been complicated far beyond the simplicity taught in the Bible. Living in God's perfect will isn't a difficult, complex thing. To the contrary, it's actually an easy thing. We know that because Jesus said so when He told us that His yoke is *easy* and His burden is light (see Matthew 11:30). Legalistic religion tries to complicate the Christ-life and make it hard to live. Jesus said that what He offers is easy.

I again remind you that this grace-based approach to walking in God's will doesn't involve a list of things you have to do. Grace is the platform from which God works, and He is the One who does what needs to be done. Our role is to completely trust Him, knowing that He will see to it that what He has planned for us will come to fruition… in His time and in His way.

Don't make the mistake of thinking that fulfilling God's will for your life isn't possible if your lifestyle—like Susannah Wesley's—seems to be a mundane, normal routine. That kind of mistake comes from a mind bogged down in faulty thinking. Every one of us can fulfill God's will for our lives right down to the minutest detail…just by relaxing and letting Christ be who He is in and through us, in the situation He has put us in. It doesn't have to be something glamorous or earth-shaking to fulfill His will for your life.

I'm reminded of Reggie Wilson, a bus driver on Metro Bus Route 48 in Seattle. Commuters who ride his bus to work each day see first-hand what can happen when a man isn't embarrassed to relax and just be who he is with confidence. Reggie is known as "the singing bus driver," and many people have attested that the enthusiasm of his heart is contagious.

It isn't uncommon to find his passengers boisterously singing "The Sunshine Song" together as they clap their hands to the beat. "If You're Happy That It's Friday, Say Uh-Huh" is a group favorite. Sometimes they are eating the cheese and crackers Reggie has put under some of the seats. "What do we do with cheese?" he asks his passengers over the bus microphone. "We share!" they respond. "That's right," Reggie answers. "Cheese is great and we don't eat it all by ourselves. We share it!"

This kind of behavior may seem eccentric or even bizarre to the analytical mind—but not to a heart set free. Reggie came under criticism when he began his routine. He thought of quitting his singing and just driving the bus. Then one day a woman who got on the bus told him, "I learned yesterday that I had terminal cancer. You made me laugh. Please don't ever stop." So he hasn't.

What is Reggie's assessment of his situation? He thinks of his job almost as a spiritual mission: "I love being a bus driver. Do you know how great it is to see a busload of smiling people? When I see that I feel like I have found my glory."*

*I have found my glory.* What do you think he means? I believe that he has discovered God's will for his life; as a driver on a Seattle city bus, Reggie White is making a difference.

Maybe you find yourself looking at your circumstances and thinking that for you to walk in the will of God is harder than for somebody who has advantages you don't see yourself possessing. Maybe you're broke. Maybe you don't have the education that others have. You may have challenging health problems. There may be other factors you see as hindering you from being able to carry out a divine plan in life.

---

* Adapted from Christine Clarridge, "No gloomy riders on Reggie Wilson's Metro bus," *Seattle Times,* February 2, 2002, accessed 1/21/09 at http://community.seattletimes.nwsource.com/archive/?date=20020202&slug=busdriver02m.

We can all find something to use as an excuse. But don't fall for the lie that you don't have the same possibilities or potential as other people. You can see the will of God realized in your life just as surely as anybody in this world can.

Let me remind you that God's plan for you is designed just for you. For that reason, it fits you perfectly. Your Father wants to lead you forward so you don't leave this world lamenting what you did or didn't do. You can live the kind of life that will point to His goodness and

> ——————
>
> Don't look at yourself and count yourself out for any reason.

grace. Our lives are to be open books telling about His faithfulness and love.

The only thing necessary for you to experience the fulfillment of what your Father has planned is to simply believe Him and start moving forward through life, acting like He is going to make it happen. Understand that your acting like you have the backing of Almighty God isn't an *act*, in the sense that you're pretending. Rather, you're *taking action* based upon what's real. The One who has called you to fulfill His plan is the same Person who will ensure that it happens.

God is on your side, and He will patiently work with you to lead you forward into the fulfillment of your destiny. Don't look at yourself and count yourself out for any reason. Don't look at your circumstances and fall into the penitentiary of excuses. Look at the One who is your very Life and put your faith in Him. No matter how weak you may think your faith is, it's enough. Just look to Him in faith, and He will do the rest. That's why it's called *grace!*

This is a new beginning. Put this book down now and charge forward with faith in your loving and sovereign Father. Don't be shaken by anything. Never give in to faithless doubting. You possess divine life, so go forth and live boldly and confidently, knowing that you *are* walking in the will of God and, because of His indwelling life, nothing—nobody—is big enough to stop you.

# About Grace Walk Ministries

IF YOU HAVE ENJOYED *Walking in the Will of God* I would be happy to hear from you and know how this grace-oriented approach to the will of God has impacted you. You can e-mail me at info@gracewalk.org or write me at the following address:

Dr. Steve McVey
Grace Walk Ministries
PO Box 3669
Riverview, FL 33568

I have developed many other resources to help you in your own grace walk. You can learn more about these on my Web site at **www .gracewalk.org.** There you will find articles, radio programs, devotions, and other information to encourage you.

If you're interested in moving to a deeper level in your study of God's grace and in your goal to share it with others, I invite you to contact me for information on becoming a Grace Walk Group Leader. A Grace Walk Group leader is different from someone heading up a G.R.A.C.E. Group, in that they are a formal part of Grace Walk Ministries. Grace Walk Group leaders facilitate small groups, guiding them through a prescribed curriculum that includes numerous audio/video and written resources I have developed. We currently have Grace Walk Groups scattered across North America and in other places around the world, and we would be happy for you to join us in our mission.

Our Father is bringing about a grace revolution within His church. If you want to be a part of that revolution by joining me in sharing the grace walk message with others, I would be happy to hear from you. Training for Grace Walk Group leadership is provided at no cost. Together we can impact the body of Christ with the liberating message of what it means to walk in freedom and grace each day.

May you be blessed as you walk in the will of God for your life each day, and as you are used by Him to share His grace with others!

# Acknowledgments

My appreciation goes to a number of people who have been a blessing to me. Some were instrumental in the making of this book. Others have nurtured my soul just by the relationship we share together.

It all started when Tim Stephenson took audio teachings I had done on knowing and doing God's will and put them in printed form, which became the seed for what you're holding in your hands now. Good job, Tim!

My wife, Melanie, has been the greatest blessing of my life in practically every way since I met her as a young teen almost 40 years ago. After all this time, she took on a new role as an amateur editor by reading the manuscript and giving me ideas that made it a better book. Melanie, my whole life would feel like one big blank page without you.

Paul Gossard is my editor at Harvest House, who has the same grace-filled DNA as me. Thanks, Paul, for catching my mistakes, suggesting improvements, and helping me think through a better way to say what I wanted to communicate. This is a much better book because of you.

Thanks goes to Abby FitzPatrick, whose courage as a young girl is as great as anybody I've seen. Abby and her parents, Kevin and Lauren, can't imagine how powerfully they prove every day that God's grace really is sufficient. I included Abby's story here because she's an amazing girl who shows just how big our God is.

Roger and Jan Dean are two friends whose journey has proven that when we keep our focus on Christ, He can unfold a plan for our lives that blesses not only us, but also everybody around us. I used their pathway as an illustration in the book because it's an example and encouragement to us all to keep trusting Him and moving forward. Cap'n, let's keep sailing forward together through life.

Appreciation is in order for the members of the Grace Walk team, who work together with me in the shared hope that God will use us to further the growing grace revolution.

Cheryl Buchanan is my Administrative Manager, who works tirelessly attending to details so I can spend my time doing what I do best. There's no way to give the credit she deserves here, but heaven knows and—I have no doubt—applauds her.

Craig Snyder is the point man for the missions outreach of our ministry and a dear friend whose enthusiasm and faith has sometimes carried me when I've felt like I was momentarily short of both.

Gerardo Vasquez is our Latin American Director, who calls me his "father in the faith." If that's true, no man could have a son of whom he is more proud.

Mike Zenker leads Grace Walk Canada and has potential like few people I know. I'm so glad he never gave up in his pursuit to work with me. He is a gift from God to me personally and to our ministry, and is a man with potential that blooms more and more every day.

Dave Lesniak manages Grace Walk Radio and is an encouraging friend who is more connected to other people than anybody I've ever met. Only eternity knows the number of people who have been impacted by God's grace through his ministry.

Mike and Julia Quarles lead Grace Walk Recovery Ministry. It's an honor for me to work with these friends. Mike was the first person I ever heard share the complete gospel of grace. God used him in my life in a profound way then and still does.

Jose Collacilli leads our ministry in Argentina. He and his wife, Stella, are a gift to their country and living proof of the message our ministry shares. It was a great day when you came on board with us, my friend.

Edwin Castellano directs Grace Walk El Salvador and is a beacon of light to the people there.

Gerardo Soberanis leads Grace Walk Mexico and calls himself my "grandson in the faith." I'm honored by the title and am thankful for how God is using him and his wife, Yamel, to change the spiritual temperature of the Mexican church.

Ken Blose has been a dear friend and has produced my video teachings for 12 years. He and Juana express the compassionate love of Christ like few people I've known.

I deeply appreciate our Grace Walk Groups Ministry leaders, whose passion to share the grace walk with others and commitment to their groups make them unsung heroes who will one day be rewarded for their labors.

For almost 20 years, Bob and Sheree Lykens have personified the true meaning of the word "friends" like nobody I've known in this life. Bob knows me better than anybody and yet we're still best friends. Wow, God is good.

My very early morning Skype talks with Paul Anderson-Walsh, my dear friend in London, England, have been one of my greatest joys in the past few years. I had wished for a brother, but didn't expect a black man in England with a strange accent. Who would have thought it?

Speaking of the English, Dave Bilbrough's music nurtured my soul through the writing of this book. What a rare breed of talent and humility. I look forward to partnering with Dave and Pat in ministry for many years to come.

Dave and Marlene Billings have been a real encouragement to me through their sense of awe over God's grace. So have Mike and Terri Williams and John and Coleen Lewis. You're all the kind of grace revolutionaries I love to work with in ministry. Let's keep spreading this grace revolution together!

If laughter truly is medicine for the soul, the fun I've had with Al and Carol Hanson has kept me healthy. Al says, "Life is too short to drink the house wine," and he motivates the rest of us to believe the same.

Ray and Laura Boatright exemplify what the grace of God can do in our lives and then through our lives as we trust Him. You two can't know how uplifting your friendship is to us.

Bill and Sarah Stewart, what could I possibly say to adequately express appreciation? Christ through you has transformed more lives than any of us could know. On behalf of a multitude in Latin America: ¡Muchisimas gracias y que Dios le bendiga! Thank you for your friendship, partnership, and encouragement through all these years.

Finally, the most important acknowledgment must go to my heavenly Father. Without Him, none of this has meaning. He is the Source and Substance of it all.

# Grace Amazing

If your Christian life seems as dry as dust and you're just going around in circles, maybe you're wandering in the wilderness. There, you feel as though...

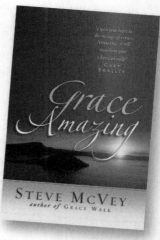

- you live by the rules, and the Bible is the rule book

- you work hard for God...but you never quite measure up

But in the land of God's amazing grace, you experience the truth that...

- God has made you alive *in Christ*— and now you want to do what He wants

- Jesus has done all the work, and you can rest in the Father's acceptance

Steve McVey reveals more of the heart of your loving, giving Father...so you can better grasp just why His grace is so amazing.

*Living in the Kingdom of God Where...*

# Grace Rules

*Are you "living by the rules"...or are you letting God's grace rule you?*

There's a big difference. If you're living *for* God—living by the rules—you'll always be exhausted. You'll feel as if you're not doing enough for Him...and that if you don't "measure up," He'll be displeased with you.

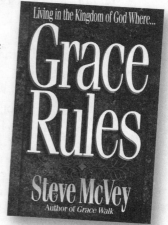

But God never meant for you to live the Christian life that way! He sent Christ to set you free from rules. He didn't call you to serve Him in your own feeble power... but to let *His* limitless power flow through you! Find out how to rest in His grace and let Him live through you in *Grace Rules*.

# Grace Walk

*What You've Always Wanted in the Christian Life*

Nothing you have ever done, nothing you could ever do, will match the incomparable joy of letting Jesus live His life through you. It is what makes the fire of passion burn so brightly in new believers. And it is what causes the light of contentment to shine in the eyes of mature believers who are growing in the grace walk.

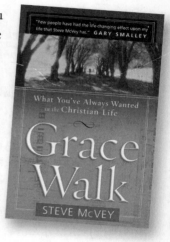

As you relax in Jesus and delight in His love and friendship, you'll find that He will do more *through you* and *in you* than you could ever do for Him or for yourself. Today is the day to let go of doing and start *being* who you are. Today is the day to start experiencing the grace walk.

# The Grace Walk Experience

*Enjoying Life the Way God Intends*

*"Make sure you're in the Word." "Have a quiet time every day." "Rededicate yourself." "Make a commitment." "Just stop sinning!"* Your frustration may be the catalyst God wants to use—right here, right now—to give you a gloriously new understanding of the Christian walk.

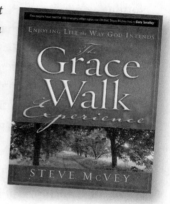

Take a deep breath and relax through eight weekly, interactive studies from Steve McVey that show you...

- why it's all right to give up on yourself and your efforts
- how to leave behind a performance- and fear-based faith
- ways to quit "doing" for God, so He can live through you
- how to view the Bible, salvation, and evangelism from a new perspective
- how to be free to enjoy God and the abundant life He's given you

Superb for small-group discussions, church classes, and individual study.

*Read a sample chapter from these or other Harvest House books at www.harvesthousepublishers.com*

# Becoming Who God Intended

*A New Picture for Your Past • A Healthy Way of Managing Your Emotions • A Fresh Perspective on Relationships*

DAVID ECKMAN

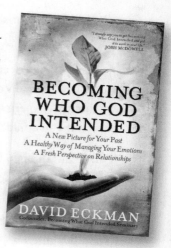

Whether you realize it or not, your imagination is filled with *pictures* of reality. The Bible indicates these pictures reveal your true "heart beliefs"—the beliefs that actually shape your everyday feelings and reactions.

David Eckman compassionately shows you how to allow God's Spirit to build new, *biblical* pictures in your heart and imagination. As you do this, you will be able to experience the life God the Father has always intended for you.

"David Eckman is a man you can trust…His teaching resonates with God's wisdom and compassion."

—**Stu Weber,** author of *Tender Warrior* and *Four Pillars of a Man's Heart*

# Knowing the Heart of the Father

*Four Experiences with God That Will Change Your Life*

DAVID ECKMAN

*You're stuffed full of Christian information. But where is God in all of it?*

Perhaps Christianity seems irrelevant to where your heart is really at. Maybe you're thirsting for a *felt experience* of the Bible's truth. What if you could…

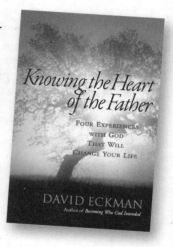

1. have an all-encompassing sense that you have a loving heavenly Dad?
2. have a sense of being enjoyed and delighted in by Him?
3. recognize that He sees you differently than you see yourself?
4. realize that *who you are* is more important to Him than *what you do?*

Do you want things to be different? See how these four great heart/soul transformations result in a vibrant, living faith that can stand up to the tests of life.